JUMBLE®

Ballet

Prance through These Pirouetting Puzzles!

**Henri Arnold,
Bob Lee,
Mike Argirion,
Jeff Knurek, &
David L. Hoyt**

TRIUMPH
BOOKS

This book is available in quantity at special discounts
for your group or organization.

For further information, contact:

Triumph Books LLC
814 North Franklin Street
Chicago, Illinois 60610
Phone: (312) 337-0747
www.triumphbooks.com

Printed in U.S.A.

ISBN: 978-1-62937-616-5

Design by Sue Knopf

Contents

JUMBLE®
Ballet

Classic Puzzles

JUMBLE

Unscramble these four Jumbles, one letter to each square, to form four ordinary words.

DROAR
☐☐○○☐

RIHAC
☐○○○☐

GUBLIN
○○☐☐☐○

MUGNIP
☐☐☐☐○○

THAT STINGY GOLFER LEFT THE CADDIE THIS.

Now arrange the circled letters to form the surprise answer, as suggested by the above cartoon.

Print answer here ○○○○○○○ THE ○○○

JUMBLE®

Unscramble these four Jumbles, one letter to each square, to form four ordinary words.

AMOFY

CUVOH

TEABED

YAARTS

We have some nice shellfish tonight

A CRUSTACEAN IS ANOTHER CREATURE THAT MIGHT HAVE THIS.

Now arrange the circled letters to form the surprise answer, as suggested by the above cartoon.

Print answer here A ⬡⬡⬡⬡ FOR A ⬡⬡⬡⬡

JUMBLE®

Unscramble these four Jumbles, one letter to each square, to form four ordinary words.

KEDAC

GWEED

SCEBIT

YEEHRB

I kinda liked that little blonde at the party

THIS KEY HAS BEEN KNOWN TO UNLOCK THE TONGUE.

Now arrange the circled letters to form the surprise answer, as suggested by the above cartoon.

Print answer here " ◯◯◯◯ – ◯◯◯ "

JUMBLE®

Unscramble these four Jumbles, one letter
to each square, to form four ordinary words.

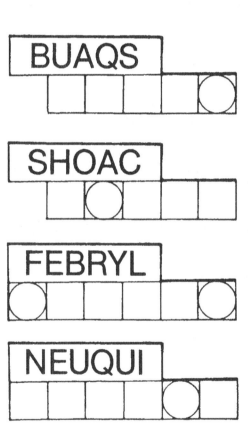

BUAQS

SHOAC

FEBRYL

NEUQUI

ONE WOMAN'S HOBBY
MIGHT BE ANOTHER
WOMAN'S THIS.

Now arrange the circled letters to form
the surprise answer, as suggested by the
above cartoon.

Print answer here

JUMBLE®

Unscramble these four Jumbles, one letter to each square, to form four ordinary words.

PEXLE

CUMIS

KELLIY

SOUTID

RUNS ACROSS THE FLOOR ALTHOUGH CAN'T WALK.

Now arrange the circled letters to form the surprise answer, as suggested by the above cartoon.

Print answer here

JUMBLE®

Unscramble these four Jumbles, one letter to each square, to form four ordinary words.

YORRS

CHALT

NECBOK

DUPLED

WHAT DAVID DECIDED TO DO WHEN GOLIATH STARTED LOOKING TIRED.

Now arrange the circled letters to form the surprise answer, as suggested by the above cartoon.

Print answer here " ⬡⬡⬡⬡ " HIM TO ⬡⬡⬡⬡⬡

JUMBLE®

Unscramble these four Jumbles, one letter
to each square, to form four ordinary words.

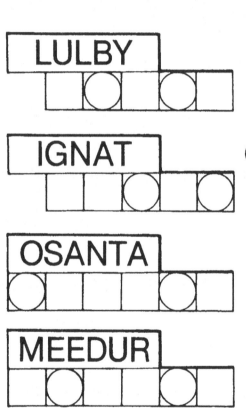

LULBY

IGNAT

OSANTA

MEEDUR

You'll love me when
I'm old and gray?

HE PROMISED
FIRST THAT HE
WOULD BE THIS.

Now arrange the circled letters to form
the surprise answer, as suggested by the
above cartoon.

Print answer here ⬡⬡⬡⬡ TO THE ⬡⬡⬡⬡

JUMBLE®

Unscramble these four Jumbles, one letter
to each square, to form four ordinary words.

EGBIE

TASHY

CUSTOC

RELOAP

A PEA-SOUPY FOG
MAY GIVE
MOTORISTS THIS.

Now arrange the circled letters to form
the surprise answer, as suggested by the
above cartoon.

Print answer here ◯◯◯ " ◯◯◯◯◯◯◯ "

JUMBLE®

Unscramble these four Jumbles, one letter
to each square, to form four ordinary words.

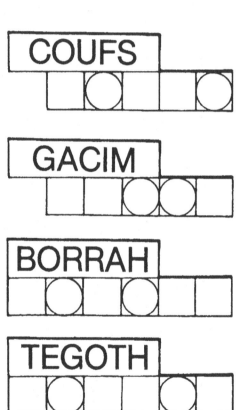

COUFS

GACIM

BORRAH

TEGOTH

You don't have to come back
after lunch

He's been
paying him
half a million
a year

MIGHT ALSO BE
"FIRED"–EVEN WHEN
SEEMINGLY THIS.

Now arrange the circled letters to form
the surprise answer, as suggested by the
above cartoon.

Print answer here ⬡ ⬡⬡⬡ " ⬡⬡⬡⬡ "

JUMBLE®

Unscramble these four Jumbles, one letter
to each square, to form four ordinary words.

YOAPS

VAMUE

THYFOR

PERTIL

I don't
approve!

You're
just
jealous

THE YOUNGER
GENERATION ALWAYS
SEEMS MORE OUT-
RAGEOUS WHEN ONE
IS NO LONGER THIS.

Now arrange the circled letters to form
the surprise answer, as suggested by the
above cartoon.

Print answer here

JUMBLE®

Unscramble these four Jumbles, one letter
to each square, to form four ordinary words.

FLOTY

CIKHT

TASSID

LAPRIL

WHAT HE GOT AS A
RESULT OF
CARELESS DRIVING.

Now arrange the circled letters to form
the surprise answer, as suggested by the
above cartoon.

Print answer here ◯ " ◯◯◯ ◯◯◯◯ "

JUMBLE®

Unscramble these four Jumbles, one letter
to each square, to form four ordinary words.

RUFOL

ZATOP

HEZEWE

VAHDLE

I got it!

There
he goes
again!

THAT WISEACRE
HAS THE SOLUTION TO
EVERY DIFFICULT
PROBLEM RIGHT
IN THIS.

Now arrange the circled letters to form
the surprise answer, as suggested by the
above cartoon.

*Print
answer
here* THE ⬡⬡⬡⬡⬡⬡ OF HIS ⬡⬡⬡⬡

JUMBLE®

Unscramble these four Jumbles, one letter
to each square, to form four ordinary words.

RANOB

CINEE

SLAVNY

POOSUR

WHAT KIND OF MARKS DID YOU
GET IN PHYSICAL EDUCATION?

Now arrange the circled letters to form
the surprise answer, as suggested by the
above cartoon.

Print
answer
here   " ◯◯◯◯ A ◯◯◯◯◯◯◯ "
                   FEW

JUMBLE.

Unscramble these four Jumbles, one letter
to each square, to form four ordinary words.

BOSEE

HUBYS

MEHRAM

NATTIC

IF HORSEBACK RIDING
BECOMES AN
"ADDICTION," THIS CAN
BE EXPENSIVE.

Now arrange the circled letters to form
the surprise answer, as suggested by the
above cartoon.

Print answer here ◯◯◯ " ◯◯◯◯◯◯ "

JUMBLE®

Unscramble these four Jumbles, one letter
to each square, to form four ordinary words.

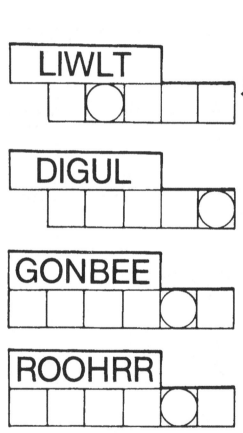

LIWLT

DIGUL

GONBEE

ROOHRR

It won't be long now.

THE GROOM WAS FIT
TO BE TIED - - -

Now arrange the circled letters to form
the surprise answer, as suggested by the
above cartoon.

Print answer here

JUMBLE®

Unscramble these four Jumbles, one letter to each square, to form four ordinary words.

UGSIE

DONUP

HINGKT

PEMEXT

They have a lot to learn

THEIR INVOLVEMENT WITH DIVING WAS ONLY THIS.

Now arrange the circled letters to form the surprise answer, as suggested by the above cartoon.

Print answer here ◯◯◯◯ - ◯◯◯◯

JUMBLE®

Unscramble these four Jumbles, one letter
to each square, to form four ordinary words.

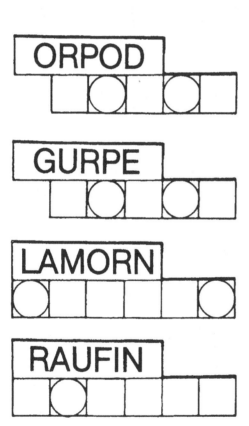

ORPOD

GURPE

LAMORN

RAUFIN

NOW IN ITS TENTH YEAR!

A THEATER OWNER
NEVER SUFFERS
IN THIS.

Now arrange the circled letters to form
the surprise answer, as suggested by the
above cartoon.

Print answer here THE " ⬡⬡⬡⬡ ⬡⬡⬡ "

JUMBLE®

Unscramble these four Jumbles, one letter
to each square, to form four ordinary words.

SEECA

TILMI

PANTIC

NORRAC

(Sniff) There goes the atmosphere again!

WHAT THOSE OLD-
FASHIONED STOCK-
YARDS USED TO
HAVE ABOUT THEM.

Now arrange the circled letters to form
the surprise answer, as suggested by the
above cartoon.

Print answer
here   A ⬡⬡⬡⬡⬡⬡⬡ " ⬡⬡⬡ "

JUMBLE®

Unscramble these four Jumbles, one letter
to each square, to form four ordinary words.

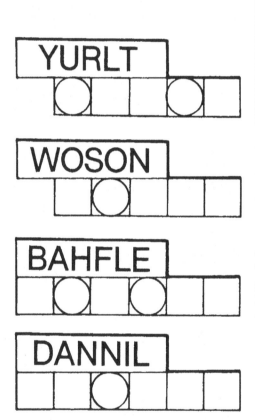

YURLT

WOSON

BAHFLE

DANNIL

WHAT MANY DRY
SPEECHES ARE.

Now arrange the circled letters to form
the surprise answer, as suggested by the
above cartoon.

Print answer here

JUMBLE®

Unscramble these four Jumbles, one letter to each square, to form four ordinary words.

YUINF

KWATE

THROOC

SNIDUM

Out of the way, you little pip-squeak

THINK BEFORE YOU SPEAK. THEN ---

Now arrange the circled letters to form the surprise answer, as suggested by the above cartoon.

Print answer here ☐☐☐ ☐☐☐'☐

21

JUMBLE®

Unscramble these four Jumbles, one letter to each square, to form four ordinary words.

ADEHA

BRUTS

TEPPIC

NAHDDE

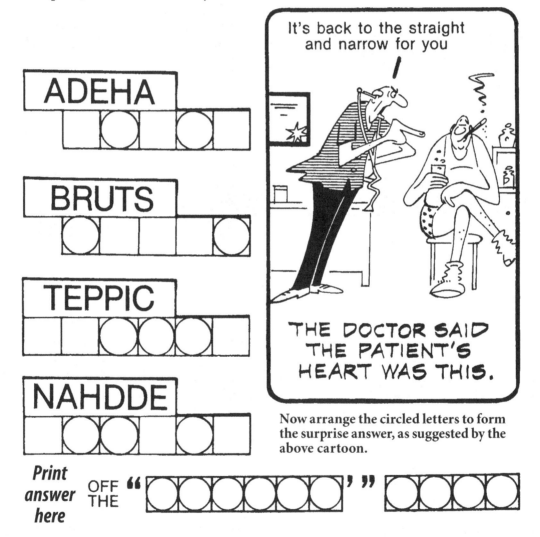

It's back to the straight and narrow for you

THE DOCTOR SAID THE PATIENT'S HEART WAS THIS.

Now arrange the circled letters to form the surprise answer, as suggested by the above cartoon.

Print answer here OFF THE " ⬡⬡⬡⬡⬡⬡ " ⬡⬡⬡⬡

JUMBLE®

Unscramble these four Jumbles, one letter
to each square, to form four ordinary words.

MAGDO

YARDT

HINGAC

TEPLES

A diet would be better

THE BEST
WEIGHT LIFTERS.

Now arrange the circled letters to form
the surprise answer, as suggested by the
above cartoon.

Print answer here

JUMBLE

Unscramble these four Jumbles, one letter
to each square, to form four ordinary words.

ULIPP

INBAC

STEGAK

CUBEKT

Yes, dear--we've already
gone over that

CLICK!

WHEN ALL IS SAID
AND DONE, SOME
PEOPLE JUST
DO THIS.

Now arrange the circled letters to form
the surprise answer, as suggested by the
above cartoon.

Print
answer
here

[   ][   ][   ][   ] ON [   ][   ][   ][   ][   ][   ][   ]

JUMBLE

Unscramble these four Jumbles, one letter
to each square, to form four ordinary words.

ETHUC

OPSOW

HIALAD

YOTHER

Everything is working out fine

HE'S THE "MASTER"
IN HIS OWN HOME
JUST SO LONG AS
HE DOES THIS.

Now arrange the circled letters to form
the surprise answer, as suggested by the
above cartoon.

Print answer here ⬡⬡⬡⬡ HE'S ⬡⬡⬡⬡

25

JUMBLE®

Unscramble these four Jumbles, one letter
to each square, to form four ordinary words.

TANGE

STUCO

RYNWIT

KEWRAH

MONEY CAN BE
LOST IN MORE THIS.

Now arrange the circled letters to form
the surprise answer, as suggested by the
above cartoon.

Print
answer
here

⬜⬜⬜⬜ ⬜⬜⬜⬜ " ⬜⬜⬜ "

26

JUMBLE®
Ballet

Daily
Puzzles

JUMBLE

Unscramble these four Jumbles, one letter
to each square, to form four ordinary words.

ALIVA

IRATT

GABLEN

MODCEY

THEY SAID THE MOVIE
HAD A HAPPY
ENDING BECAUSE
EVERYONE WAS THIS.

Now arrange the circled letters to form
the surprise answer, as suggested by the
above cartoon.

Print answer here ☐☐☐☐☐ IT WAS ☐☐☐☐☐

JUMBLE®

Unscramble these four Jumbles, one letter
to each square, to form four ordinary words.

RINED

AMDAM

GELIGG

HAPNOR

WHAT THAT ECCENTRIC
DOOR-TO-DOOR
SALESMAN MUST
HAVE BEEN.

Now arrange the circled letters to form
the surprise answer, as suggested by the
above cartoon.

Print answer
here   " ⬡⬡⬡⬡ – ⬡⬡⬡⬡ "

JUMBLE®

Unscramble these four Jumbles, one letter
to each square, to form four ordinary words.

REVUC

TAWLZ

SCULIE

BUTSOE

HE DINES WITH
THE UPPER SET,
AND IS APT TO
DO THIS, TOO.

Now arrange the circled letters to form
the surprise answer, as suggested by the
above cartoon.

Print answer here ◯◯◯ HIS ◯◯◯◯◯◯◯

JUMBLE

Unscramble these four Jumbles, one letter
to each square, to form four ordinary words.

INGAR

TUMOH

LOUBED

HERITH

WHAT THE GUY WHO
WAS HER "IDEAL"
BECAME AFTER THEY
GOT MARRIED.

Now arrange the circled letters to form
the surprise answer, as suggested by the
above cartoon.

Print answer here

JUMBLE®

Unscramble these four Jumbles, one letter
to each square, to form four ordinary words.

VOLEH

DUGIE

AFAIRS

TELRUT

He's
a
nut

WHY HE TOOK
THE SCREENS OFF
HIS WINDOWS.

Now arrange the circled letters to form
the surprise answer, as suggested by the
above cartoon.

*Print
answer
here*   TO ⬡⬡⬡ THE ⬡⬡⬡⬡⬡ ⬡⬡⬡

JUMBLE®

Unscramble these four Jumbles, one letter to each square, to form four ordinary words.

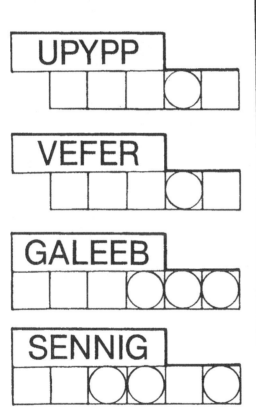

UPYPP

VEFER

GALEEB

SENNIG

Guess I'll turn in

THE ONLY TIME THAT CROOK'S ON THE LEVEL IS WHEN HE'S THIS.

Now arrange the circled letters to form the surprise answer, as suggested by the above cartoon.

Print answer here

33

JUMBLE®

Unscramble these four Jumbles, one letter
to each square, to form four ordinary words.

GREBA

RAUZE

DEBBAL

LEWLOY

Ten years!
Next case!

HE WANTED TO
BECOME A LAWYER
BADLY, BUT HE ENDED
UP BECOMING THIS.

Now arrange the circled letters to form
the surprise answer, as suggested by the
above cartoon.

Print answer here   A

JUMBLE

Unscramble these four Jumbles, one letter to each square, to form four ordinary words.

PYKER

LOJYL

SARGYS

ENVELE

(Sob) I'll never speak to him again!

ANY MAN WHO ARGUES WITH HIS WIFE AND WINS---

Now arrange the circled letters to form the surprise answer, as suggested by the above cartoon.

Print answer here

JUMBLE®

Unscramble these four Jumbles, one letter to each square, to form four ordinary words.

RIVOY

THIGE

VIEWEL

DAMNET

Guess I made an idiot of myself last night

WHEN YOU "LIVE IT UP," YOU MIGHT TRY TO DO THIS AFTERWARDS.

Now arrange the circled letters to form the surprise answer, as suggested by the above cartoon.

Print answer here

JUMBLE®

Unscramble these four Jumbles, one letter
to each square, to form four ordinary words.

YASES

LASIE

GIBNEN

TYGODS

WHERE MANY
FLIERS MAY GET
THEIR BASIC
TRAINING.

Now arrange the circled letters to form
the surprise answer, as suggested by the
above cartoon.

Print answer here

JUMBLE®

Unscramble these four Jumbles, one letter
to each square, to form four ordinary words.

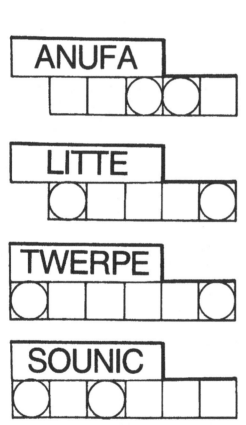

ANUFA

LITTE

TWERPE

SOUNIC

LOOK OUT FOR
THIS WHEN
APPROACHING A
FORK IN THE ROAD.

Now arrange the circled letters to form
the surprise answer, as suggested by the
above cartoon.

Print answer here A

JUMBLE®

Unscramble these four Jumbles, one letter
to each square, to form four ordinary words.

RADIC

ALOCK

SNUFIL

LUTTUM

STOP!!

ONE DOESN'T
RUN AFTER THIS.

Now arrange the circled letters to form
the surprise answer, as suggested by the
above cartoon.

Print answer here THE ☐☐☐☐ ☐☐☐☐☐

JUMBLE®

Unscramble these four Jumbles, one letter to each square, to form four ordinary words.

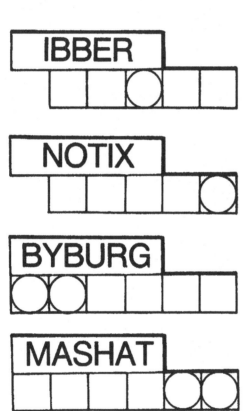

IBBER

NOTIX

BYBURG

MASHAT

Excellent

THIS IS RIGHT
WHEN IT'S LEFT
ON BOTH SIDES.

Now arrange the circled letters to form the surprise answer, as suggested by the above cartoon.

Print answer here A

JUMBLE®

Unscramble these four Jumbles, one letter to each square, to form four ordinary words.

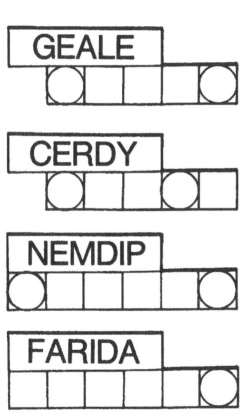

GEALE

CERDY

NEMDIP

FARIDA

WHAT AN INEXPERIENCED RIDER MIGHT GET WHEN HE FALLS OFF A HORSE.

Now arrange the circled letters to form the surprise answer, as suggested by the above cartoon.

Print answer here

41

JUMBLE®

Unscramble these four Jumbles, one letter
to each square, to form four ordinary words.

ZACER

KLANE

LOYMED

TURBLE

YOU DON'T
APPRECIATE THE
USEFULNESS OF
THIS UNTIL YOU
USE IT UP.

Now arrange the circled letters to form
the surprise answer, as suggested by the
above cartoon.

Print answer here

JUMBLE

Unscramble these four Jumbles, one letter
to each square, to form four ordinary words.

NOLFE

SAUME

YORPTS

BURNEM

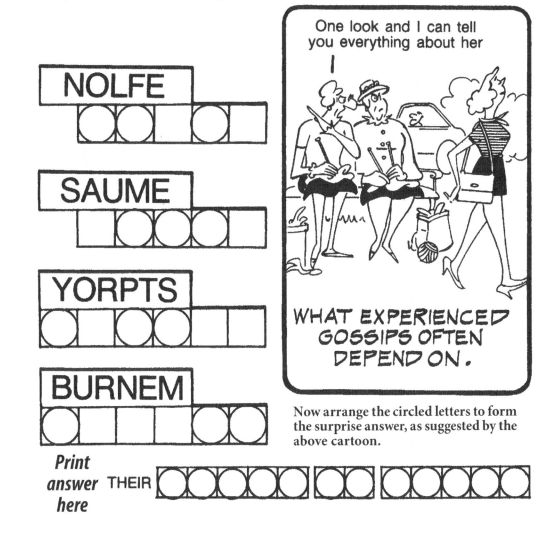

One look and I can tell
you everything about her

WHAT EXPERIENCED
GOSSIPS OFTEN
DEPEND ON.

Now arrange the circled letters to form
the surprise answer, as suggested by the
above cartoon.

Print
answer   THEIR
here

JUMBLE®

Unscramble these four Jumbles, one letter
to each square, to form four ordinary words.

KARCC

MYKOS

LORCAR

TEKLET

WHY THE ESCAPED
CON ON THE LAM
TOOK A JOB
ON THE RAILROAD.

Now arrange the circled letters to form
the surprise answer, as suggested by the
above cartoon.

Print answer here TO [ ][ ][ ][ ] [ ][ ][ ][ ][ ][ ]

JUMBLE®

Unscramble these four Jumbles, one letter
to each square, to form four ordinary words.

BECAL

RADAW

FRASIA

CLINPE

WHAT THE ROYAL
PARENT WAS
TEMPTED TO CALL
HIS NEWBORN HEIR.

Now arrange the circled letters to form
the surprise answer, as suggested by the
above cartoon.

Print
answer
here

◯◯◯◯◯◯ OF " ◯◯◯◯◯ "

JUMBLE®

Unscramble these four Jumbles, one letter
to each square, to form four ordinary words.

DORRA

BOESE

MERRIP

DOBOLY

The game's not over!

I'm quitting!

WHAT A DIETER
WITHOUT WILL
POWER IS.

Now arrange the circled letters to form
the surprise answer, as suggested by the
above cartoon.

Print answer here A ⬡⬡⬡⬡ ⬡⬡⬡⬡⬡

JUMBLE®

Unscramble these four Jumbles, one letter
to each square, to form four ordinary words.

MICER

FRASC

SHEERA

NAIGAN

HOW THE ENGLISH-
MAN DESCRIBED
HIS WIFE'S DRIVING.

Now arrange the circled letters to form
the surprise answer, as suggested by the
above cartoon.

Print answer here " ⬡⬡⬡⬡⬡⬡⬡⬡ ! "

JUMBLE®

Unscramble these four Jumbles, one letter
to each square, to form four ordinary words.

DUIHM

THIRM

REFUGI

YIELDE

WHAT THE
NEWLYWED MUSIC
LOVERS PLEDGED
EACH OTHER.

Now arrange the circled letters to form
the surprise answer, as suggested by the
above cartoon.

Print answer here

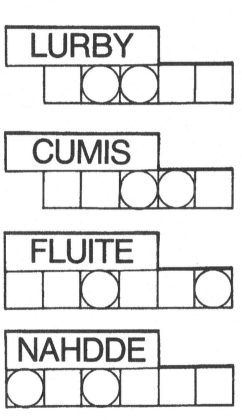

JUMBLE®

Unscramble these four Jumbles, one letter to each square, to form four ordinary words.

LURBY

CUMIS

FLUITE

NAHDDE

HOW THE POTTER MAKES HIS LIVING.

Now arrange the circled letters to form the surprise answer, as suggested by the above cartoon.

Print answer here

JUMBLE®

Unscramble these four Jumbles, one letter
to each square, to form four ordinary words.

GRABE

KLAYN

HIGLES

TIPECK

WHAT A
PESSIMIST MIGHT
EXPECT TO GET ON
A SILVER PLATTER.

Now arrange the circled letters to form
the surprise answer, as suggested by the
above cartoon.

Print answer here

JUMBLE®

Unscramble these four Jumbles, one letter
to each square, to form four ordinary words.

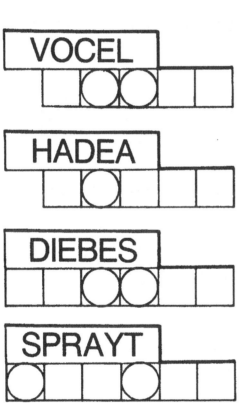

VOCEL

HADEA

DIEBES

SPRAYT

WHAT THE PLAY-
WRIGHT TURNED
GARDENER
WORKED ON.

Now arrange the circled letters to form
the surprise answer, as suggested by the
above cartoon.

Print answer here ⟨◯◯◯ ◯◯◯◯◯⟩

51

JUMBLE

Unscramble these four Jumbles, one letter
to each square, to form four ordinary words.

TISUE

CREYM

RATVAC

WHOALL

WHAT THE BASE-
BALL PLAYER
TURNED ORCHESTRA
LEADER HAD
TO KNOW.

Now arrange the circled letters to form
the surprise answer, as suggested by the
above cartoon.

Print answer here

JUMBLE®

Unscramble these four Jumbles, one letter
to each square, to form four ordinary words.

VALIA

WORBE

MEHRAM

LEWBIA

HOW YOU MIGHT
ANNOUNCE THE
BIRTH OF A SON TO
YOUR FRIENDS.

Now arrange the circled letters to form
the surprise answer, as suggested by the
above cartoon.

Print answer
here BY "◯◯◯◯" ◯◯◯◯

JUMBLE®

Unscramble these four Jumbles, one letter to each square, to form four ordinary words.

GIMAC

TORNS

CAHBLE

RESPON

WHAT SHE SAID WHEN HE YELLED AT HER ABOUT THE MONEY SHE SPENT ON A CASHMERE COAT.

Now arrange the circled letters to form the surprise answer, as suggested by the above cartoon.

Print answer here "◯◯'◯ ◯◯◯◯ ◯◯◯◯!"

JUMBLE®

Unscramble these four Jumbles, one letter to each square, to form four ordinary words.

TIMAD

CHITH

GREESY

UNTEAR

WHAT THE HORSE THOUGHT HIS WIFE LOOKED LIKE AS SHE PREPARED FOR BED.

Now arrange the circled letters to form the surprise answer, as suggested by the above cartoon.

Print answer here A ⬡⬡⬡⬡⬡ – ⬡⬡⬡⬡

JUMBLE®

Unscramble these four Jumbles, one letter
to each square, to form four ordinary words.

RUMON

HUBYS

TUMONT

GEULED

WHAT THE BORED
PERCUSSION PLAYER
THOUGHT HIS
WORK WAS.

Now arrange the circled letters to form
the surprise answer, as suggested by the
above cartoon.

Print answer here

JUMBLE®

Unscramble these four Jumbles, one letter
to each square, to form four ordinary words.

RAAMO

POSOT

BYSUIL

SEMIED

WHAT THE LOWEST
VOICE IN THE PRISON
QUARTET WAS.

Now arrange the circled letters to form
the surprise answer, as suggested by the
above cartoon.

Print answer
here   A

JUMBLE®

Unscramble these four Jumbles, one letter
to each square, to form four ordinary words.

LYDOM

DATUL

SPOLGE

RICHEP

WHAT THE BUTCHER'S
SON HAD WHEN HIS
DAD GOT LOCKED
IN THE REFRIGERATOR.

Now arrange the circled letters to form
the surprise answer, as suggested by the
above cartoon.

Print answer here   A ☐☐☐☐☐ ☐☐☐

JUMBLE®

Unscramble these four Jumbles, one letter
to each square, to form four ordinary words.

LAHCK

SEHCS

DOYLIB

NOPPIL

WHERE WAS THE
FISH WHEN THE
KID PLAYING HOOKY
CAUGHT HIM?

Now arrange the circled letters to form
the surprise answer, as suggested by the
above cartoon.

Print answer here

JUMBLE®

Unscramble these four Jumbles, one letter to each square, to form four ordinary words.

UPMEL

TAIMY

CADETH

NAULCY

WHAT THE WAITER DID WHEN ASKED HOW THE SEA-FOOD WAS.

Now arrange the circled letters to form the surprise answer, as suggested by the above cartoon.

Print answer here   HE

JUMBLE®

Unscramble these four Jumbles, one letter
to each square, to form four ordinary words.

ADURF

ESTAE

RUINJY

ROUGAC

WHAT THE ROMANTIC
SPANIARD PICKED IN
HIS SWEETHEART'S
GARDEN.

Now arrange the circled letters to form
the surprise answer, as suggested by the
above cartoon.

Print answer here

JUMBLE®

Unscramble these four Jumbles, one letter
to each square, to form four ordinary words.

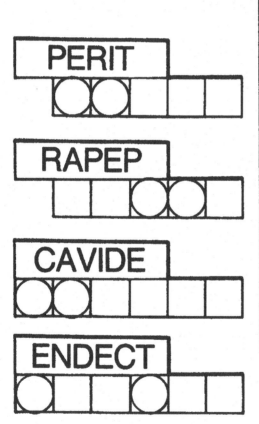

PERIT

RAPEP

CAVIDE

ENDECT

BEFORE | AFTER

HOW HAIR THAT
WAS PARTED
YESTERDAY MAY
APPEAR TODAY.

Now arrange the circled letters to form
the surprise answer, as suggested by the
above cartoon.

Print answer here

JUMBLE®

Unscramble these four Jumbles, one letter to each square, to form four ordinary words.

CORUS

GUJED

HUNCAL

STAPOL

WHAT THE COMICAL SURGEON WAS.

Now arrange the circled letters to form the surprise answer, as suggested by the above cartoon.

Print answer here   AN ⬡⬡⬡ ⬡⬡⬡⬡⬡

JUMBLE®

Unscramble these four Jumbles, one letter
to each square, to form four ordinary words.

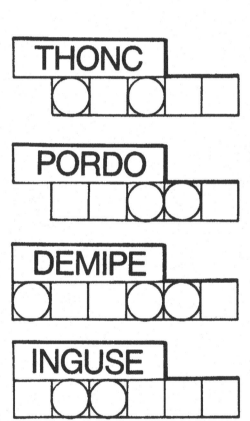

THONC

PORDO

DEMIPE

INGUSE

WHAT THE NECKTIE
SALESMEN DID AT
THEIR CONVENTION.

Now arrange the circled letters to form
the surprise answer, as suggested by the
above cartoon.

Print answer here

JUMBLE.

Unscramble these four Jumbles, one letter
to each square, to form four ordinary words.

FLAYE

HOTBO

FACEEF

SAWURL

Sunny
all day

WHAT WEATHER
FORECASTERS
SOMETIMES ARE.

Now arrange the circled letters to form
the surprise answer, as suggested by the
above cartoon.

Print answer here

65

JUMBLE®

Unscramble these four Jumbles, one letter
to each square, to form four ordinary words.

MYLAD

ZAMIE

STINCH

ENTODE

WHAT THE HAY
FEVER SUFFERER
DID WHEN HE
READ ABOUT THE
POLLEN COUNT.

Now arrange the circled letters to form
the surprise answer, as suggested by the
above cartoon.

Print answer
here

JUMBLE®

Unscramble these four Jumbles, one letter
to each square, to form four ordinary words.

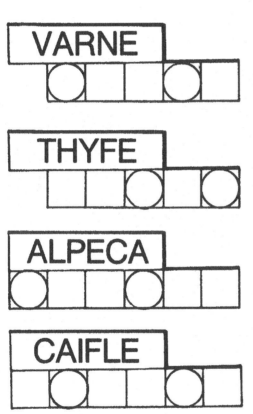

VARNE
◯◯☐◯◯

THYFE
☐◯◯◯

ALPECA
◯☐☐◯☐☐

CAIFLE
☐◯☐☐◯☐

WHAT THE
SEASONED COMMUTER
TRIES WHEN HE
FORGETS HIS TICKET.

Now arrange the circled letters to form
the surprise answer, as suggested by the
above cartoon.

Print answer here " ◯◯◯◯ ◯◯◯◯ "

67

JUMBLE®

Unscramble these four Jumbles, one letter to each square, to form four ordinary words.

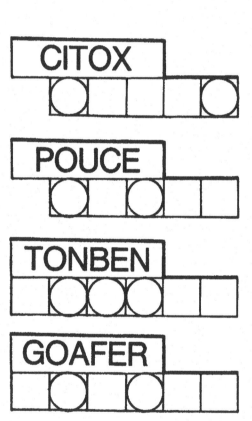

CITOX

POUCE

TONBEN

GOAFER

TELLER

ANOTHER NAME FOR A CHECK FORGER.

Now arrange the circled letters to form the surprise answer, as suggested by the above cartoon.

Print answer here A ☐☐ - ☐☐☐☐☐☐☐

JUMBLE

Unscramble these four Jumbles, one letter to each square, to form four ordinary words.

LULBY

CARPH

LUFNIX

BASHUM

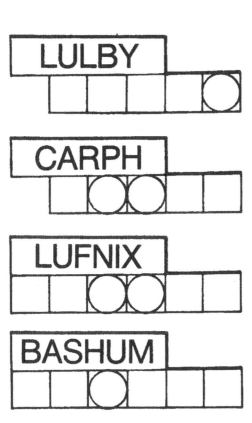

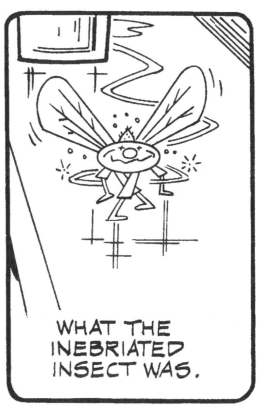

WHAT THE INEBRIATED INSECT WAS.

Now arrange the circled letters to form the surprise answer, as suggested by the above cartoon.

Print answer here A

JUMBLE®

Unscramble these four Jumbles, one letter
to each square, to form four ordinary words.

VEFER

AXORB

TARREY

PEESLY

WHAT THE RED-
CAP WHO WENT
INTO FOREIGN
TRADE WAS.

Now arrange the circled letters to form
the surprise answer, as suggested by the
above cartoon.

Print answer here AN ◯◯ – ◯◯◯◯◯◯◯

JUMBLE®

Unscramble these four Jumbles, one letter
to each square, to form four ordinary words.

ORMUF

NISOB

TOLBEG

OKOCIE

WHAT HAPPENED
WHEN THE THER-
MOMETER FELL ON
A HOT DAY?

Now arrange the circled letters to form
the surprise answer, as suggested by the
above cartoon.

Print answer here

JUMBLE®

Unscramble these four Jumbles, one letter
to each square, to form four ordinary words.

NAGIT

YOANG

BANACA

CORCUN

WHAT THE FRENCH
CABARET DANCER
KEPT INSISTING.

Now arrange the circled letters to form
the surprise answer, as suggested by the
above cartoon.

*Print answer
here*

JUMBLE®

Unscramble these four Jumbles, one letter to each square, to form four ordinary words.

YASSA

GEDUN

THARRE

HARTTO

ALWAYS CHEERED WHEN THEY'RE DOWN AND OUT.

Now arrange the circled letters to form the surprise answer, as suggested by the above cartoon.

Print answer here

JUMBLE

Unscramble these four Jumbles, one letter
to each square, to form four ordinary words.

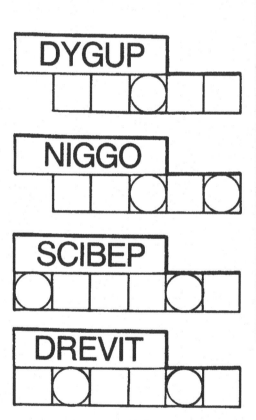

DYGUP

NIGGO

SCIBEP

DREVIT

HE HOPED TO MAKE
A BIG SPLASH WITH
THE LADIES BUT
TURNED OUT TO
BE THIS.

Now arrange the circled letters to form
the surprise answer, as suggested by the
above cartoon.

Print answer here A

JUMBLE®

Unscramble these four Jumbles, one letter
to each square, to form four ordinary words.

OUMID

SUHOE

GREFOT

YOUTCH

WHAT THE SHOE
MERCHANT DID
ABOUT HIS BILLS.

Now arrange the circled letters to form
the surprise answer, as suggested by the
above cartoon.

Print answer here HE ◯◯◯◯◯◯ ◯◯◯◯

JUMBLE®

Unscramble these four Jumbles, one letter
to each square, to form four ordinary words.

JYTET

YORFT

SENTOL

REFOBE

HOW THE TENDER-
FOOT FELT AFTER
HIS FIRST DAY ON
HORSEBACK.

Now arrange the circled letters to form
the surprise answer, as suggested by the
above cartoon.

Print answer here

JUMBLE®

Unscramble these four Jumbles, one letter
to each square, to form four ordinary words.

RANOB

THALC

WEFTES

WAHGIE

WHAT THE
WEREWOLF SAID
WHEN SHE ASKED
FOR MINK.

Now arrange the circled letters to form
the surprise answer, as suggested by the
above cartoon.

Print answer here " ⬡⬡⬡⬡ ⬡⬡⬡⬡ ! "

JUMBLE

Unscramble these four Jumbles, one letter to each square, to form four ordinary words.

LELOH

YARIF

GURDED

BEIMIB

WHAT THE PASSENGERS DID TO THE CONDUCTOR WHEN THE TRAIN WAS LATE.

Now arrange the circled letters to form the surprise answer, as suggested by the above cartoon.

Print answer " ☐☐☐☐☐☐ " AT ☐☐☐
here

JUMBLE®

Unscramble these four Jumbles, one letter
to each square, to form four ordinary words.

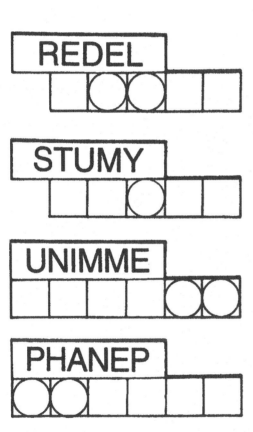

REDEL

STUMY

UNIMME

PHANEP

THEY MAKE
HOLDUPS EASIER.

Now arrange the circled letters to form
the surprise answer, as suggested by the
above cartoon.

Print answer here

JUMBLE®

Unscramble these four Jumbles, one letter
to each square, to form four ordinary words.

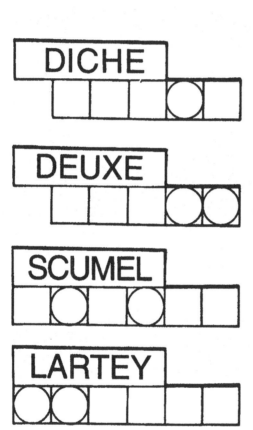

DICHE

DEUXE

SCUMEL

LARTEY

THE KIND OF
CLOTHES YOU MIGHT
BUY AFTER YOU'VE
LOST WEIGHT.

Now arrange the circled letters to form
the surprise answer, as suggested by the
above cartoon.

Print answer here "⬡⬡⬡⬡⬡⬡⬡"

JUMBLE®

Unscramble these four Jumbles, one letter
to each square, to form four ordinary words.

YACKT

YOHEN

CHANIG

LUPPER

Thank goodness my
wife is rich!

PINK
SLIP

THIS COULD SAVE
A HIGH-UP FROM
A PAINFUL
COMEDOWN.

Now arrange the circled letters to form
the surprise answer, as suggested by the
above cartoon.

Print answer here A

JUMBLE®

Unscramble these four Jumbles, one letter to each square, to form four ordinary words.

VACHO

NUMIS

BLATUR

TISMEY

It HAD been so peaceful!

A LOUD CRY THAT'S QUIET TO START WITH.

Now arrange the circled letters to form the surprise answer, as suggested by the above cartoon.

Print answer here "  "

JUMBLE®

Unscramble these four Jumbles, one letter to each square, to form four ordinary words.

KONET

BYLUR

NECTED

SADLIM

I bought this with my prize money

HOME
SITES
FOR
SALE

WHAT THE LOTTERY-WINNING REALTOR CONSIDERED HIS PROPERTY PURCHASE.

Now arrange the circled letters to form the surprise answer, as suggested by the above cartoon.

Print answer here " ◯◯◯◯ " OF ◯◯◯◯

JUMBLE

Unscramble these four Jumbles, one letter
to each square, to form four ordinary words.

USTEA

VUCER

FEBRYL

CEVIED

WHEN THEY WATCHED
THE STEELWORKERS
THE CROWD WAS----

Now arrange the circled letters to form
the surprise answer, as suggested by the
above cartoon.

Print answer here

JUMBLE®

Unscramble these four Jumbles, one letter
to each square, to form four ordinary words.

KLACH

VOPER

GREFOT

ROHORR

You're on in ten minutes

STAGE
DOOR

He never misses
a performance

WHAT THE COP
MOONLIGHTING AS AN
ACTOR WAS KNOWN AS.

Now arrange the circled letters to form
the surprise answer, as suggested by the
above cartoon.

Print answer
here A ☐☐☐☐☐ ☐☐☐☐☐☐☐☐

JUMBLE®

Unscramble these four Jumbles, one letter
to each square, to form four ordinary words.

SUBGO

EMICH

FLORGE

INDUPT

Wait for the pistol!

WHAT THE RUNNER
WANTED TO GET
A JUMP ON.

Now arrange the circled letters to form
the surprise answer, as suggested by the
above cartoon.

Print answer here THE ◯◯◯◯◯◯◯◯

JUMBLE®

Unscramble these four Jumbles, one letter
to each square, to form four ordinary words.

NAHEY

TAMEL

CHUPIC

DUSSIC

Something's missing

I'll fix that

THIS CAN RESCUE
A MEAL WHEN ALL
ELSE FAILS.

Now arrange the circled letters to form
the surprise answer, as suggested by the
above cartoon.

Print answer here ⬡⬡⬡⬡ , IN A ⬡⬡⬡⬡⬡

JUMBLE®

Unscramble these four Jumbles, one letter
to each square, to form four ordinary words.

TUMOH

FRYOT

DANGIR

LEESAW

Does he write them all himself?

AUTHORING
SPOOKY STORIES
MADE HIM THIS.

Now arrange the circled letters to form
the surprise answer, as suggested by the
above cartoon.

Print
answer A "〇〇〇〇〇" 〇〇〇〇〇〇〇
here

JUMBLE®

Unscramble these four Jumbles, one letter
to each square, to form four ordinary words.

INBAC

TUCOL

REECCO

SIMYAD

BANK

Now we can get a
tan in the sun

WHY THE BANK
ROBBERS HEADED FOR
THE SEASHORE.

Now arrange the circled letters to form
the surprise answer, as suggested by the
above cartoon.

Print
answer
here

THE ⬡⬡⬡⬡⬡ WAS ⬡⬡⬡⬡⬡

JUMBLE®

Unscramble these four Jumbles, one letter
to each square, to form four ordinary words.

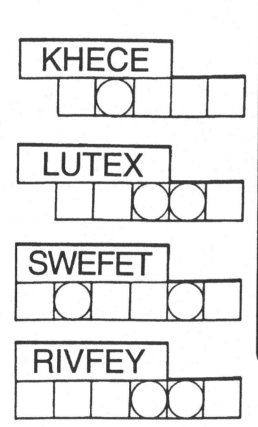

KHECE

LUTEX

SWEFET

RIVFEY

I can't believe it

HOW HE FELT
WHEN HIS CAR
RAN OUT OF GAS.

Now arrange the circled letters to form
the surprise answer, as suggested by the
above cartoon.

Print answer here

JUMBLE®

Unscramble these four Jumbles, one letter
to each square, to form four ordinary words.

LITRL

DUXEE

DARFIA

BILDOY

So THAT'S who he's
been dating!

WHAT THE LANDSCAPER
UNCOVERED IN THE
ROYAL GARDEN.

Now arrange the circled letters to form
the surprise answer, as suggested by the
above cartoon.

Print answer here THE ⬡⬡⬡⬡ ⬡⬡⬡⬡

JUMBLE®

Unscramble these four Jumbles, one letter
to each square, to form four ordinary words.

KLEAF

GELEY

RALCOR

TURIAL

They sing so
beautifully

WHAT THE
BIRDS GAVE THE
NATURE LOVERS.

Now arrange the circled letters to form
the surprise answer, as suggested by the
above cartoon.

Print answer here A

JUMBLE®

Unscramble these four Jumbles, one letter
to each square, to form four ordinary words.

YANGO

BUDOT

SMABAL

GEDDUR

THE PURSE SNATCHER'S
FAVORITE ACTIVITY
AT A PARTY.

Now arrange the circled letters to form
the surprise answer, as suggested by the
above cartoon.

Print answer here THE ⬡⬡⬡⬡ ⬡⬡⬡

JUMBLE®

Unscramble these four Jumbles, one letter
to each square, to form four ordinary words.

ORPOD

CYKAT

ENOMAY

PLOATS

Fifty cents...guaranteed
to make you look younger

PEOPLE WHO BELIEVE IN
THE FOUNTAIN OF YOUTH
GET THIS.

Now arrange the circled letters to form
the surprise answer, as suggested by the
above cartoon.

Print answer here

JUMBLE®

Unscramble these four Jumbles, one letter
to each square, to form four ordinary words.

DYPUG

TYMIA

RAHWTT

INDOOM

Can't make up
their minds

AN AMBITIOUS COWBOY'S
LIFE IS FILLED
WITH THIS.

Now arrange the circled letters to form
the surprise answer, as suggested by the
above cartoon.

**Print answer
here** ◯◯◯◯◯◯◯ AND ◯◯◯◯◯

JUMBLE

Unscramble these four Jumbles, one letter
to each square, to form four ordinary words.

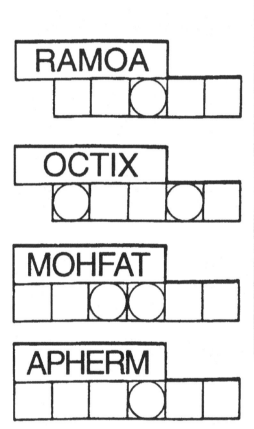

RAMOA

OCTIX

MOHFAT

APHERM

WHAT THE WELL-
TO-DO STOCKBROKER
GAVE THE MAITRE D'.

Now arrange the circled letters to form
the surprise answer, as suggested by the
above cartoon.

Print answer here A

JUMBLE®

Unscramble these four Jumbles, one letter
to each square, to form four ordinary words.

BLEEL

LANVA

THINCS

MALFEE

Stop, thief!

WHAT THE COPS
CONSIDERED THE
STRONG-ARM ROBBER.

Now arrange the circled letters to form
the surprise answer, as suggested by the
above cartoon.

Print answer here A ⬡⬡⬡ OF ⬡⬡⬡⬡⬡

JUMBLE®

Unscramble these four Jumbles, one letter
to each square, to form four ordinary words.

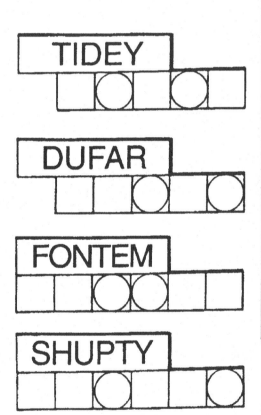

TIDEY

DUFAR

FONTEM

SHUPTY

You can't lick the system

POST OFFICE

WHAT THE POST
OFFICE EXPERIENCES
WHEN RATES ARE
ABOUT TO GO UP.

Now arrange the circled letters to form
the surprise answer, as suggested by the
above cartoon.

Print answer here A ⬡⬡⬡⬡⬡ — ⬡⬡⬡

JUMBLE®

Unscramble these four Jumbles, one letter
to each square, to form four ordinary words.

That looks
like a
good spot

Gosh--I
don't know

SERCS

WROPE

FAINAR

GOURAC

WHY THE PILOT
COULDN'T DECIDE
WHERE TO LAND.

Now arrange the circled letters to form
the surprise answer, as suggested by the
above cartoon.

Print answer here HE ☐☐☐ ☐☐ IN THE ☐☐☐

JUMBLE®

Unscramble these four Jumbles, one letter to each square, to form four ordinary words.

ZYZID

IKYTT

VETOMI

PROPHE

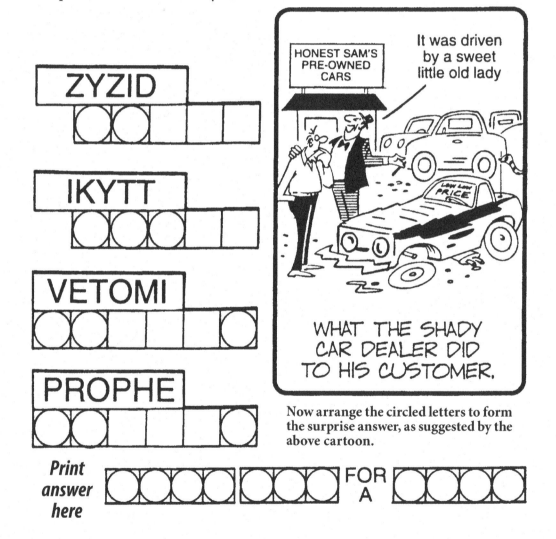

HONEST SAM'S PRE-OWNED CARS

It was driven by a sweet little old lady

WHAT THE SHADY CAR DEALER DID TO HIS CUSTOMER.

Now arrange the circled letters to form the surprise answer, as suggested by the above cartoon.

Print answer here

⬡⬡⬡⬡ ⬡⬡⬡ FOR A ⬡⬡⬡⬡

JUMBLE®

Unscramble these four Jumbles, one letter
to each square, to form four ordinary words.

ICHED

MYDAL

MANDET

RANTTY

I'm here to fix the sink

WHAT THE ELEGANTLY
DRESSED REPAIRMAN
WAS KNOWN AS.

Now arrange the circled letters to form
the surprise answer, as suggested by the
above cartoon.

Print answer here A ☐☐☐☐☐☐ ☐☐☐☐☐

JUMBLE®

Unscramble these four Jumbles, one letter
to each square, to form four ordinary words.

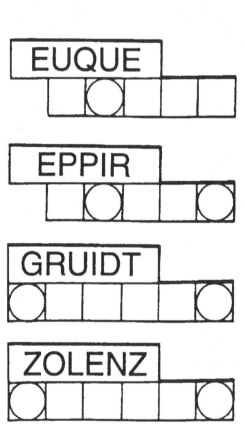

EUQUE

EPPIR

GRUIDT

ZOLENZ

He's worked hard
all his life

HOW THE COFFEE
SHOP OWNER MADE
HIS MONEY.

Now arrange the circled letters to form
the surprise answer, as suggested by the
above cartoon.

Print answer here HE

JUMBLE®

Unscramble these four Jumbles, one letter
to each square, to form four ordinary words.

GALDE

ZOMGI

TISDEG

KENVIO

I'm wasting my talent here. I should be writing songs, not moving dirt.

Get to work!

HE GOT A JOB BUILDING A
MOAT, BUT HE WASN'T ----

Now arrange the circled letters to form
the surprise answer, as suggested by the
above cartoon.

Print answer here

JUMBLE

Unscramble these four Jumbles, one letter to each square, to form four ordinary words.

RUBYL

SNATD

CIVONE

TEPICO

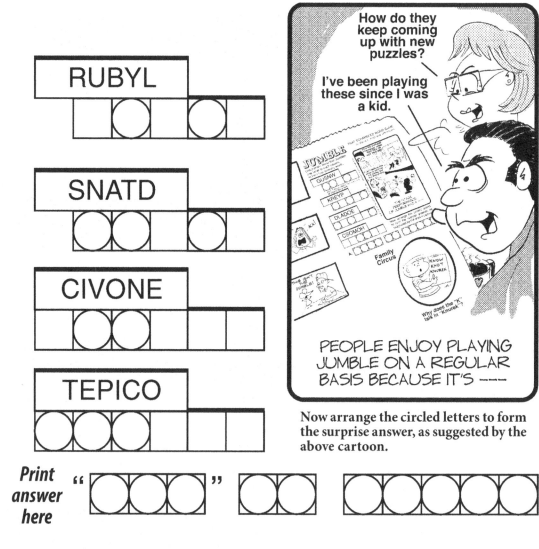

How do they keep coming up with new puzzles?

I've been playing these since I was a kid.

PEOPLE ENJOY PLAYING JUMBLE ON A REGULAR BASIS BECAUSE IT'S ----

Now arrange the circled letters to form the surprise answer, as suggested by the above cartoon.

Print answer here " ☐☐☐ " ☐☐ ☐☐☐☐☐

JUMBLE®

Unscramble these four Jumbles, one letter to each square, to form four ordinary words.

TYEPT

KUNJY

MASYDI

CUPENO

Ewww!

HE WANTED TO GET THE SKUNK OUT OF THE GARAGE, BUT THE SKUNK ----

Now arrange the circled letters to form the surprise answer, as suggested by the above cartoon.

Print answer here

JUMBLE

Unscramble these four Jumbles, one letter
to each square, to form four ordinary words.

ALDIV

SREPS

CNISTH

PULBAR

HE WANTED TO OPEN A JUNKYARD IN THE NEIGHBORHOOD, BUT HE HAD TO ---

Now arrange the circled letters to form
the surprise answer, as suggested by the
above cartoon.

Print answer here

JUMBLE

Unscramble these four Jumbles, one letter
to each square, to form four ordinary words.

CACOH

HYTEF

SOPIGS

TRIPOM

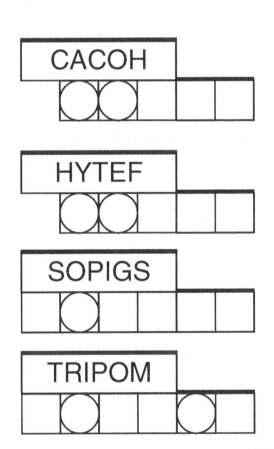

I just need five more dollars to buy some bells for my band.

She still owes me $10.

Me, too!

THE COW WHO WAS
ALWAYS BORROWING
MONEY WAS A ----

Now arrange the circled letters to form
the surprise answer, as suggested by the
above cartoon.

Print answer here

JUMBLE®

Unscramble these four Jumbles, one letter to each square, to form four ordinary words.

TODAP

NILCG

CEFINT

BENTON

We need to pack it up and go. We can eat at home.

TRYING TO EAT OUTSIDE WITH A THUNDERSTORM APPROACHING WAS ----

Now arrange the circled letters to form the surprise answer, as suggested by the above cartoon.

Print answer here

JUMBLE®

Unscramble these four Jumbles, one letter
to each square, to form four ordinary words.

GUYGM

WITAA

NOYELL

RISEMY

I can't believe you finished so fast.

Yep. Ahead of schedule. Enjoy!

THE CONSTRUCTION OF
THEIR NEW POOL HAD
GONE ---

Now arrange the circled letters to form
the surprise answer, as suggested by the
above cartoon.

Print answer here

JUMBLE

Unscramble these four Jumbles, one letter
to each square, to form four ordinary words.

ROWNS

DUHIM

GOTOES

DOLCED

Cup of joe, Rocky.

About time you woke up.

Right away, Hoot.

THESE BIRDS OF PREY MET
LATE IN THE EVENING
BECAUSE THEY WERE ----

Now arrange the circled letters to form
the surprise answer, as suggested by the
above cartoon.

JUMBLE®

Unscramble these four Jumbles, one letter to each square, to form four ordinary words.

RAWEY

LENTK

TUNMOT

CAFTEF

Mooove over.
Time for the
Funky Chicken.

It has nothing to do
with the shoes.
You can't dance.

These new
shoes must
not fit me.

THE CLUMSY HORSE DIDN'T
DO WELL AT THE DANCE
CLASS BECAUSE HE HAD ----

Now arrange the circled letters to form the surprise answer, as suggested by the above cartoon.

JUMBLE®

Unscramble these four Jumbles, one letter
to each square, to form four ordinary words.

TONMH

WLRIH

BUTODI

JENGAL

Has my table
called to say
if they were
coming?

No calls. They
should have
been here.

RESERVED

THE TABLE HAD BEEN
RESERVED FOR A PARTY OF
EIGHT, AND THE WAITRESS
WAS ---

Now arrange the circled letters to form
the surprise answer, as suggested by the
above cartoon.

JUMBLE®

Unscramble these four Jumbles, one letter to each square, to form four ordinary words.

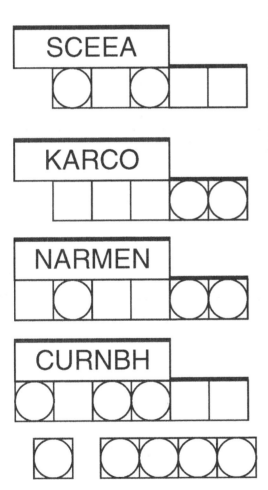

SCEEA

KARCO

NARMEN

CURNBH

I love fresh corn. I'll take five.

It's fresh all right. That will be $5.

CORN

HOW MUCH DID THE PIRATE PAY FOR THE CORN?

Now arrange the circled letters to form the surprise answer, as suggested by the above cartoon.

JUMBLE®

Unscramble these four Jumbles, one letter to each square, to form four ordinary words.

KALYE

LADYM

GUDYOH

BARJEB

We made a special menu item just for you.

I hope it's something spicy.

Clever!

The Red Lion
Today's Special
PRIMHS
HENCKIC
ECRI
UAGSESA
EPREPSP
NONOI

WHEN THE "PUNNY" PUZZLE MAKERS WENT OUT TO EAT, THEY ENJOYED THE ----

Now arrange the circled letters to form the surprise answer, as suggested by the above cartoon.

" ◯◯◯◯◯◯ - ◯◯◯ "

JUMBLE®

Unscramble these four Jumbles, one letter
to each square, to form four ordinary words.

CYREM

TILTE

BARETT

WUDINN

I don't think things can get worse.

Your spending is way too destructive. I'm out of here!

CHARGING SO MANY THINGS
ON HIS CREDIT CARD
WAS ---

Now arrange the circled letters to form
the surprise answer, as suggested by the
above cartoon.

Print answer here " ◯◯◯◯-◯◯◯◯◯◯◯◯◯◯ "

JUMBLE®

Unscramble these four Jumbles, one letter to each square, to form four ordinary words.

NAKEL
○○○□□

SOKDU
○□□○○

PUTEYD
○○□○□□

YONWAH
□□□□○○

Rosie will only tell you the recipe if you're ready.

I'm not sure I trust him.

THE BREAD COMPANY'S TOP SECRET RECIPE WAS ----

Now arrange the circled letters to form the surprise answer, as suggested by the above cartoon.

Print answer here " ○○○○○ " ○○ ○○○○

116

JUMBLE®

Unscramble these four Jumbles, one letter
to each square, to form four ordinary words.

MIOCC

HENTT

SINHIF

GEPDEL

I like the wrought
iron, but the chain
link is cheaper.

So, what do
you think?

I can't
decide.

SALE

WHEN IT CAME TO CHOOSING
WROUGHT IRON OR CHAIN
LINK, THEY WERE ----

Now arrange the circled letters to form
the surprise answer, as suggested by the
above cartoon.

Print
answer
here

JUMBLE®

Unscramble these four Jumbles, one letter
to each square, to form four ordinary words.

SVOHE

GINGO

TEKTIC

UNEVEA

Wow! Traffic
is really bad
for a Monday.

I'm
out of
tissues.

THE DRIVER, WITH THE BAD
COLD, WASN'T HAPPY WITH
ALL THE ----

Now arrange the circled letters to form
the surprise answer, as suggested by the
above cartoon.

*Print
answer
here*

JUMBLE®

Unscramble these four Jumbles, one letter to each square, to form four ordinary words.

CRIPE

GANYT

SWOMID

HESKNA

We'd better hurry or you'll miss your plane.

I'm not finished visiting my daughter.

HE WAS HOPING HIS MOTHER-IN-LAW WOULD BE LEAVING TODAY, BUT SHE HAD ----

Now arrange the circled letters to form the surprise answer, as suggested by the above cartoon.

Print answer here

JUMBLE®

Unscramble these four Jumbles, one letter
to each square, to form four ordinary words.

NURKT

TAHEW

MOYLOG

NOYTBU

It's the perfect style for us.

I'd love the view of the rim every day.

THE NEW ONE-STORY HOUSE FOR SALE AT THE BOTTOM OF THE GRAND CANYON WAS A ———

Now arrange the circled letters to form
the surprise answer, as suggested by the
above cartoon.

Print answer here

JUMBLE®

Unscramble these four Jumbles, one letter
to each square, to form four ordinary words.

CIYKP

NOYHE

CUTSAC

CURDEE

There's only room
for two of you!

WHEN THE HEN BOUGHT THE
NEW TWO-DOOR SPORTS
CAR, SHE BOUGHT A ----

Now arrange the circled letters to form
the surprise answer, as suggested by the
above cartoon.

*Print
answer
here*

" "

PUZZLE
120

JUMBLE®

Unscramble these four Jumbles, one letter
to each square, to form four ordinary words.

YINRA

GUYMG

WEYIRN

TARTHO

THE DOG JUST COULDN'T
FINISH CHEWING THE WHOLE
BONE, AND IT WAS ---

Now arrange the circled letters to form
the surprise answer, as suggested by the
above cartoon.

Print
answer
here

JUMBLE®

Unscramble these four Jumbles, one letter
to each square, to form four ordinary words.

ACEDY

NAYIR

GONVIL

ABIBDE

HE COULDN'T AFFORD A LOT
OF PROPERTY TO GROW
WINE GRAPES, SO HE
SETTLED FOR A ---

Now arrange the circled letters to form
the surprise answer, as suggested by the
above cartoon.

Print answer here ⬡⬡⬡⬡ - ⬡⬡⬡⬡

123

JUMBLE

Unscramble these four Jumbles, one letter to each square, to form four ordinary words.

DOYLD

LIROB

REZEFE

CUTAFE

No one was hurt. This mess is all that's left.

Do you have any crackers?

AFTER THE EXPLOSION AT THE FRENCH CHEESE FACTORY, THERE WAS ----

Now arrange the circled letters to form the surprise answer, as suggested by the above cartoon.

Print answer here

◯ ◯◯◯ ◯◯ " ◯◯ - ◯◯◯◯ "

JUMBLE®

Unscramble these four Jumbles, one letter to each square, to form four ordinary words.

TUCEA

VEIRR

BHGITL

LEDILA

Now this is my kind of party.

This is the only tradition from England I still like.

You know, if this were cold, it might be very refreshing.

AFTER GAINING INDEPENDENCE FROM BRITAIN, THEIR FAVORITE BEVERAGE WAS ----

Now arrange the circled letters to form the surprise answer, as suggested by the above cartoon.

Print answer " ⃝⃝⃝⃝⃝ - ⃝⃝⃝ "
here

JUMBLE

Unscramble these four Jumbles, one letter
to each square, to form four ordinary words.

DEWEG

NURDO

CCYATH

GULENJ

I think we're set.
Take us down.
Sound the diving
alarm!

Aye, aye, sir!

THE SUBMARINE WAS BRAND-
NEW AND THE CAPTAIN WAS
ANXIOUS TO ---

Now arrange the circled letters to form
the surprise answer, as suggested by the
above cartoon.

PUZZLE

125

JUMBLE

Unscramble these four Jumbles, one letter to each square, to form four ordinary words.

WEHYC

SINMU

XCSEES

DORNTE

I made them especially for you.

I've never seen anything like these!

HE WANTED HIS GLASSES TO BE UNLIKE ANYONE ELSE'S, SO HE HAD A PAIR ----

Now arrange the circled letters to form the surprise answer, as suggested by the above cartoon.

" ☐☐☐☐☐☐ - ☐☐☐☐ - ☐☐ "

JUMBLE®

Unscramble these four Jumbles, one letter
to each square, to form four ordinary words.

NATYG

SYEDE

TRAMET

PAALPE

Your secretary is
going to love
one of these.

Which one do
I get?

THE POPULARITY OF WORD
PROCESSORS IN THE 1960S,
LED TO ---

Now arrange the circled letters to form
the surprise answer, as suggested by the
above cartoon.

*Print answer
here*

JUMBLE®

Unscramble these four Jumbles, one letter
to each square, to form four ordinary words.

OSUHE

FOYLT

ARDILA

OKIREO

Isn't she wonderful?

We can get two "Bettys" for you.

EVERYTHING $1

They don't sell this here!

EVERYTHING $1

BARBIE WAS EXPENSIVE, SO
THEY HOPED SHE'D SETTLE
FOR THE ---

Now arrange the circled letters to form
the surprise answer, as suggested by the
above cartoon.

Print
answer
here

" ⬡⬡⬡⬡ - ⬡⬡⬡ " ⬡⬡⬡⬡⬡

JUMBLE®

Unscramble these four Jumbles, one letter
to each square, to form four ordinary words.

DALIP

YELCC

STIMIF

BAHMSU

We're not
going to be
lost out here,
are we?

Why
aren't we
moving?

Relax!
We'll be
fine.

WHEN THE WIND STOPPED, HE
TOLD EVERYONE ON THE
SAILBOAT TO ---

Now arrange the circled letters to form
the surprise answer, as suggested by the
above cartoon.

Print answer here

JUMBLE®

Unscramble these four Jumbles, one letter
to each square, to form four ordinary words.

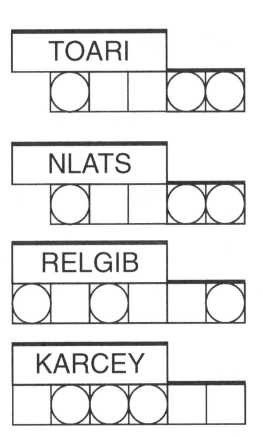

TOARI

NLATS

RELGIB

KARCEY

Shall we set a
course for the
Talosian system?

Yes. Let's
explore
every
corner of
our galaxy.

ON THE SCI-FI
SHOW, THE MILKY
WAY HAD A ----

Now arrange the circled letters to form
the surprise answer, as suggested by the
above cartoon.

*Print
answer
here*

JUMBLE®

Unscramble these four Jumbles, one letter to each square, to form four ordinary words.

LHYYS

PUTRE

WANDRO

TRUUFE

So, in this closet I keep my out-of-season clothes.

AISLE 1

SPRING HATS

SUMMER HATS

SPRING SHOES
SUMMER SHOES

FALL SWEATERS

WINTER SWEATERS

SHE HAD SO MANY CLOTHES, THAT HER HOME LOOKED LIKE A ----

Now arrange the circled letters to form the surprise answer, as suggested by the above cartoon.

Print answer " ◯◯◯◯ - ◯◯◯◯◯ "
here

JUMBLE®

Unscramble these four Jumbles, one letter to each square, to form four ordinary words.

LERBE

GIRDI

TACNAV

ULDNOA

Let's pretend we're measuring the circumference of an orange again.

But it's so much bigger.

Π × DIAMETER = 2 × Π × RADIUS

CIRCUMFERENCE
DIAMETER
RADIUS

WHEN IT CAME TO MEASURING THE EARTH'S CIRCUMFERENCE, THERE WAS A ---

Now arrange the circled letters to form the surprise answer, as suggested by the above cartoon.

Print answer here

JUMBLE

Unscramble these four Jumbles, one letter
to each square, to form four ordinary words.

HISSU

KYNID

PERILT

LAMFEE

Hey, buddy,
I'll bug him
by flying
around.

All right, pal,
and I'll bug
him on the
floor.

THE HOUSEFLY AND
THE COCKROACH
WERE ––

Now arrange the circled letters to form
the surprise answer, as suggested by the
above cartoon.

*Print
answer
here*

" ⃝⃝⃝⃝ " ⃝⃝⃝⃝⃝⃝⃝⃝

JUMBLE

Unscramble these four Jumbles, one letter
to each square, to form four ordinary words.

DERLE

LOFDO

LAXHEE

PLOFYP

Aren't you the
sweetest little
thing!

Granny, you
know what?
I love you.
That's what.

GRANNY SMITH'S
GRANDSON WAS
THE ---

Now arrange the circled letters to form
the surprise answer, as suggested by the
above cartoon.

*Print
answer
here*

JUMBLE

Unscramble these four Jumbles, one letter to each square, to form four ordinary words.

SMUYT

VOIME

WITERR

ACEDFA

What's that wonderful smell?

It's called "Bullseye" cologne.

It makes me quiver.

THE ARCHER'S NEW COLOGNE WAS ---

Now arrange the circled letters to form the surprise answer, as suggested by the above cartoon.

Print answer here " ☐☐☐☐☐ - ☐☐☐☐☐ "

JUMBLE

Unscramble these four Jumbles, one letter
to each square, to form four ordinary words.

NNOKW

INOON

IKWEDC

ONISCA

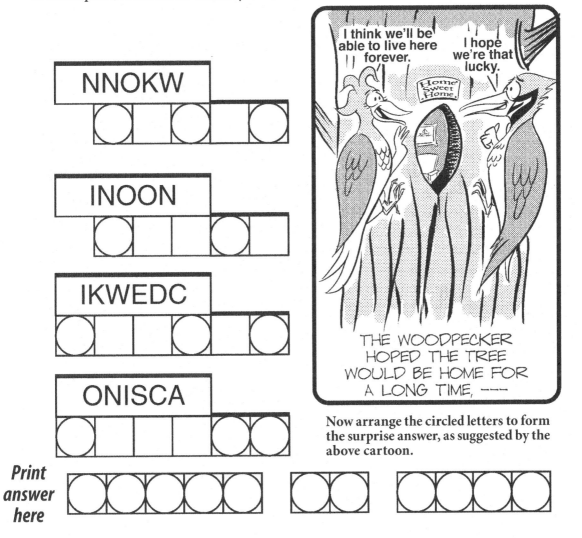

I think we'll be able to live here forever.

I hope we're that lucky.

Home Sweet Home

THE WOODPECKER HOPED THE TREE WOULD BE HOME FOR A LONG TIME, ----

Now arrange the circled letters to form
the surprise answer, as suggested by the
above cartoon.

Print answer here

137

JUMBLE

Unscramble these four Jumbles, one letter to each square, to form four ordinary words.

CIYKP

INKEF

ONKYDE

TUTELO

Stevie! I got you the Clouseau part!

I can't believe I get to follow Peter Sellers!

WHEN STEVE MARTIN GOT THE ROLE OF INSPECTOR CLOUSEAU, HE WAS ----

Now arrange the circled letters to form the surprise answer, as suggested by the above cartoon.

Print answer here

JUMBLE®

Unscramble these four Jumbles, one letter
to each square, to form four ordinary words.

USAHQ

TURET

ONEHGU

GYTIZL

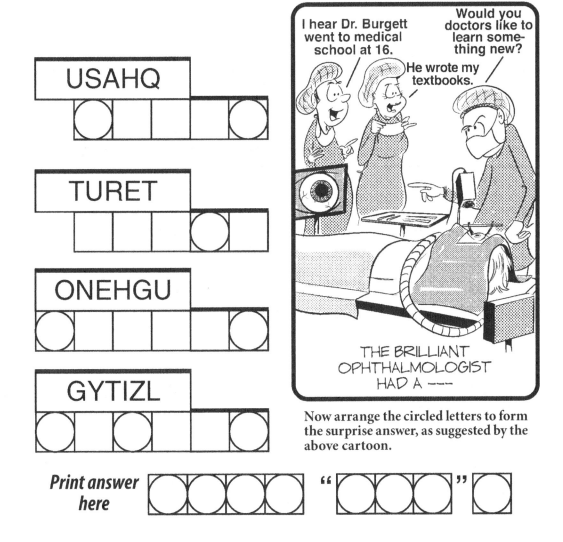

I hear Dr. Burgett
went to medical
school at 16.

Would you
doctors like to
learn some-
thing new?

He wrote my
textbooks.

THE BRILLIANT
OPHTHALMOLOGIST
HAD A ----

Now arrange the circled letters to form
the surprise answer, as suggested by the
above cartoon.

**Print answer
here**   ⬡⬡⬡⬡ " ⬡⬡⬡ " ⬡

JUMBLE®

Unscramble these four Jumbles, one letter to each square, to form four ordinary words.

DUNEU

SUHIS

PURBTA

LOHOAP

Didn't you take my class 10 years ago?

I haven't painted since.

SHE HADN'T PAINTED IN YEARS, SO SHE TOOK A CLASS TO ----

Now arrange the circled letters to form the surprise answer, as suggested by the above cartoon.

Print answer here

JUMBLE®

Unscramble these four Jumbles, one letter to each square, to form four ordinary words.

FIWTS

GETAN

BOAAEM

RYLUSE

WHEN THE SCUBA DIVER STARTLED THE OCTOPUS, IT PUT HIM ----

Now arrange the circled letters to form the surprise answer, as suggested by the above cartoon.

Print answer here

[ ] [ ] " [ ] [ ] [ ] [ ] " [ ] [ ] [ ]

JUMBLE®

Unscramble these four Jumbles, one letter
to each square, to form four ordinary words.

UNOCE

LIHEW

ALPEDD

SOBBAR

How about
that view? The
Canyon's about
a mile deep!

Wow!

It's a
long
way
down.

THEIR TOUR OF THE GRAND
CANYON BEGAN WITH THEIR
GUIDE SAYING ----

Now arrange the circled letters to form
the surprise answer, as suggested by the
above cartoon.

Print
answer
here

JUMBLE®

Unscramble these four Jumbles, one letter to each square, to form four ordinary words.

RISUV

LITTE

NAAABC

IRRRMO

How many Super Bowls have you won? Zero!

Are you ready to lose?

We're not worried.

Very funny, Cheese-head.

GATE 12

WHEN FANS FROM OPPOSING TEAMS GOT OFF THE PLANE, IT WAS ---

Now arrange the circled letters to form the surprise answer, as suggested by the above cartoon.

Print answer here

"☐-☐☐☐☐☐" ☐☐☐☐

JUMBLE®

Unscramble these four Jumbles, one letter to each square, to form four ordinary words.

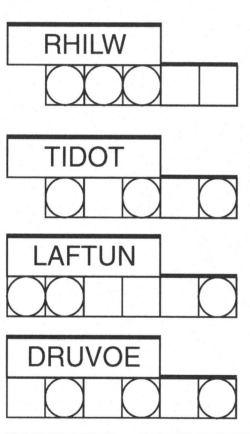

RHILW

TIDOT

LAFTUN

DRUVOE

It looks perfect! So many tasty workers!

I've had my eye on this planet for a while.

ALIENS DECIDED TO TAKE OVER EARTH BECAUSE THEY THOUGHT ----

Now arrange the circled letters to form the surprise answer, as suggested by the above cartoon.

Print answer here

JUMBLE®

Unscramble these four Jumbles, one letter
to each square, to form four ordinary words.

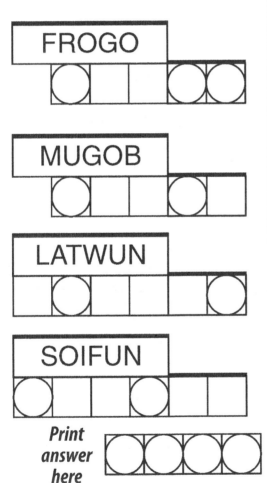

FROGO

MUGOB

LATWUN

SOIFUN

May I get this wrapped, please?

I've been a Jumble fan for 30 years. You know who would love this Jumble calendar? My mom!

THE TALKATIVE PERSON
WRAPPING CHRISTMAS
PRESENTS AT THE MALL
HAD THE ----

Now arrange the circled letters to form
the surprise answer, as suggested by the
above cartoon.

*Print
answer
here*

JUMBLE

Unscramble these four Jumbles, one letter to each square, to form four ordinary words.

ANYHE

GUOLM

LUBNED

AACREM

What a great harvest.

Our profits are going to grow this year.

WHEN IT CAME TO MAKING MONEY SELLING GRAPES, THE GROWER ———

Now arrange the circled letters to form the surprise answer, as suggested by the above cartoon.

Print answer here

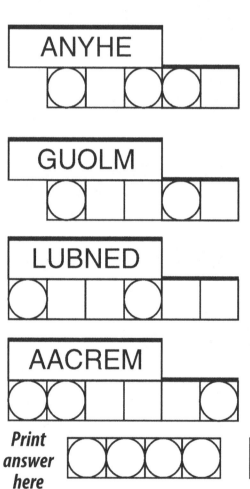

JUMBLE®

Unscramble these four Jumbles, one letter
to each square, to form four ordinary words.

NTKAH

DEGNU

MAREYC

DASILM

I've never seen anyone better.

He's much nicer than that McEnroe chap.

ONCE RANKED #1 FOR 302 STRAIGHT WEEKS, ROGER FEDERER WAS ----

Now arrange the circled letters to form
the surprise answer, as suggested by the
above cartoon.

Print answer here

JUMBLE

Unscramble these four Jumbles, one letter
to each square, to form four ordinary words.

KLIYS

ZLTIG

MURNEB

NORDAP

We're reading.
Leave us alone, or
I'll turn you into a
frog!

What does
that say?

"HARRY POTTER" FANS
COULDN'T PUT THE BOOKS
DOWN, FINDING THEM ----

Now arrange the circled letters to form
the surprise answer, as suggested by the
above cartoon.

**Print
answer
here**

JUMBLE®

Unscramble these four Jumbles, one letter to each square, to form four ordinary words.

NGATR

EDAHA

LIDOYB

EARMID

What do I have to do to get you to buy this car?

We want it at cost. Plus, we want free GPS.

And more for our trade-in.

AFTER TEST-DRIVING THE CAR, THEY WERE READY TO DRIVE A ---

Now arrange the circled letters to form the surprise answer, as suggested by the above cartoon.

Print answer here

149

JUMBLE®

Unscramble these four Jumbles, one letter to each square, to form four ordinary words.

TAAPD

XCATE

DAMIDY

DIMELD

This prosciutto-wrapped melon is amazing!

This is a local favorite.

Every meal has been great!

I know!

Grazie!

CAFE ROMA

WITH GREAT RESTAURANTS IN MILAN, FLORENCE AND ROME, THEY ENJOYED THEIR TRIP TO ---

Now arrange the circled letters to form the surprise answer, as suggested by the above cartoon.

Print answer here " ◯◯◯◯◯◯ "

JUMBLE®

Unscramble these four Jumbles, one letter
to each square, to form four ordinary words.

RILEN

AUGTM

TTALET

REFTER

SHE COULDN'T EAT ANOTHER
BITE, AND EVERYONE ELSE
WAS IN ----

Now arrange the circled letters to form
the surprise answer, as suggested by the
above cartoon.

Print answer here

JUMBLE

Unscramble these four Jumbles, one letter
to each square, to form four ordinary words.

GERME

GOMIZ

WEYLEK

TYNPAR

With these
ships, we can
control the
Mediterranean.

And then the
world.

WHEN ANCIENT ITALIANS BUILT
HUMAN-POWERED WARSHIPS,
THEY CREATED A ----

Now arrange the circled letters to form
the surprise answer, as suggested by the
above cartoon.

*Print
answer
here*

" ☐☐☐ - ☐☐☐ " ☐☐☐☐☐☐☐

JUMBLE®

Unscramble these four Jumbles, one letter
to each square, to form four ordinary words.

CATHL

CAWTH

LELNOY

AYEWEL

Wow! People
are everywhere!

WHEN THE CARPET STORE
HAD A HUGE SALE,
CUSTOMERS WERE ----

Now arrange the circled letters to form
the surprise answer, as suggested by the
above cartoon.

Print
answer
here

◯◯◯◯ - ◯◯ - ◯◯◯◯

JUMBLE

Unscramble these four Jumbles, one letter
to each square, to form four ordinary words.

LIRGL

SMIKP

CADEFA

CNOMUL

THE NUMBER OF
CUSTOMERS ROSE AT
THE SKYDIVING SCHOOL,
THANKS TO THEIR ----

Now arrange the circled letters to form
the surprise answer, as suggested by the
above cartoon.

*Print
answer
here*

JUMBLE®

Unscramble these four Jumbles, one letter
to each square, to form four ordinary words.

SLOFS

GAMIE

LMINEB

RVOFRE

WITH PLANES LANDING ONE
AFTER ANOTHER, THE SKY
WAS FILLED WITH ----

Now arrange the circled letters to form
the surprise answer, as suggested by the
above cartoon.

Print answer here

JUMBLE

Unscramble these four Jumbles, one letter
to each square, to form four ordinary words.

CTEFH

ITODI

RAWDON

FITNAN

I thought of you when this came in.

I've been looking for one of these for years.

HE WANTED TO EXPAND HIS COLLECTION, AND THE MESOPOTAMIAN ABACUS WOULD MAKE A ----

Now arrange the circled letters to form
the surprise answer, as suggested by the
above cartoon.

Print answer here

JUMBLE®

Unscramble these four Jumbles, one letter
to each square, to form four ordinary words.

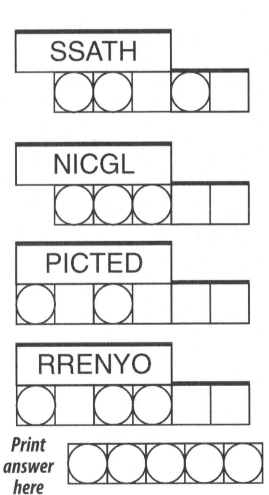

SSATH

NICGL

PICTED

RRENYO

THE LUMBERJACK COULD
CHOP THROUGH A PIECE
OF WOOD IN A ---

Now arrange the circled letters to form
the surprise answer, as suggested by the
above cartoon.

Print
answer
here

JUMBLE.

Unscramble these four Jumbles, one letter to each square, to form four ordinary words.

OYMAF

PENTI

TBREET

DTAUSJ

THEY WERE ABLE TO SET UP AT THE CAMPGROUND AFTER PAYING AN ----

Now arrange the circled letters to form the surprise answer, as suggested by the above cartoon.

Print answer here " ◯◯◯◯◯ - ◯◯◯◯◯ " ◯◯◯

JUMBLE®

Unscramble these four Jumbles, one letter to each square, to form four ordinary words.

VOSHE

KUHNC

LEYCER

XNBIOG

So, are you interested?

That's why I'm here. I've done the research, and I know what I'll pay.

NO ONE TOLD HER WHAT TO PURCHASE. SHE DID HER OWN RESEARCH AND WAS THERE ----

Now arrange the circled letters to form the surprise answer, as suggested by the above cartoon.

Print answer "◯◯◯" here ◯◯◯◯◯◯◯

JUMBLE

Unscramble these four Jumbles, one letter
to each square, to form four ordinary words.

RMICP

YONAN

LONELP

CTUBEK

SHE GREW AND HARVESTED
HER OWN FOOD BECAUSE
SHE WAS A ---

Now arrange the circled letters to form
the surprise answer, as suggested by the
above cartoon.

Print
answer
here

JUMBLE®

Unscramble these four Jumbles, one letter to each square, to form four ordinary words.

VAROB

BUDTO

NIYTEN

GOLUNE

I'm tired

What do you say we just stay here for a while?

THE AFRICAN FELINES WERE EXHAUSTED AFTER A LONG DAY AND WERE JUST ----

Now arrange the circled letters to form the surprise answer, as suggested by the above cartoon.

Print answer here

"◯◯◯◯" ◯◯◯◯◯◯

JUMBLE®

Unscramble these four Jumbles, one letter to each square, to form four ordinary words.

ALOCK

BOMOL

MERAKB

RVOMEE

HE REMEMBERED INVENTING THE "DRAM" COMPUTER CHIP IN 1968 BECAUSE IT WAS ----

Now arrange the circled letters to form the surprise answer, as suggested by the above cartoon.

Print answer here ◯◯◯◯◯◯◯◯◯

JUMBLE® Ballet

Challenger Puzzles

JUMBLE®

Unscramble these six Jumbles, one letter to each square, to form six ordinary words.

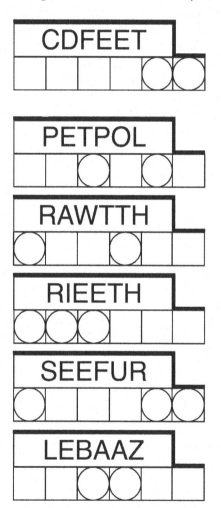

CDFEET

PETPOL

RAWTTH

RIEETH

SEEFUR

LEBAAZ

BUY YOUR STAMPS TODAY.

SAME DAY DELIVERY AVAILABLE

PRIORITY MAIL SUPPLIES HERE.

May I help you?

Can I get this to the committee on the Hill today?

How much for a stamp?

THE POST OFFICE IN WASHINGTON, D.C. FEATURED ---

Now arrange the circled letters to form the surprise answer, as suggested by the above cartoon.

Print answer here

JUMBLE®

Unscramble these six Jumbles, one letter to each square, to form six ordinary words.

YEMMAH

DOHSUL

RAGCIL

SEFWET

TEINNY

REMTAK

TIPPIE, HOYT &

Wow! What an honor.

Welcome aboard, Kent. We'll get you your parking spot.

Put it there, partner. We'll see you at the club.

WHEN THE ATTORNEY BECAME A PARTNER, HE RECEIVED ---

Now arrange the circled letters to form the surprise answer, as suggested by the above cartoon.

Print answer here

JUMBLE®

Unscramble these six Jumbles, one letter to each square, to form six ordinary words.

PAYCON

LANLOG

ALDROL

SIREYM

CANPER

STEMDO

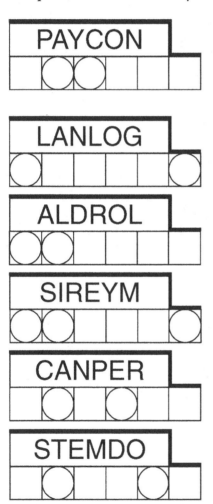

Dad! We made you breakfast in bed! Can we go fishing? Can we have pizza?

Let's all eat. Then, we'll figure out something.

What's the plan?

HE ENJOYED BEING A FATHER ALL WEEK LONG, BUT HE WAS ESPECIALLY ENJOYING ---

Now arrange the circled letters to form the surprise answer, as suggested by the above cartoon.

Print answer here

" ◯◯◯ - ◯◯◯ " ◯◯◯◯◯◯◯◯

PUZZLE

164

JUMBLE®

Unscramble these six Jumbles, one letter to each square, to form six ordinary words.

SSHALP

HENBID

INPUDA

LETRAL

SNITIS

SENSUL

I love this one every time I see it. I've seen it 10 times. Hey, you kinda dance like Elaine.

Ha ha. Very funny, you "hipster doofus." I love these reruns.

THE TV SHOW "SEINFELD" HAS BEEN SO SUCCESSFUL IN SYNDICATION THANKS TO ---

Now arrange the circled letters to form the surprise answer, as suggested by the above cartoon.

Print answer here

JUMBLE

Unscramble these six Jumbles, one letter to each square, to form six ordinary words.

NECACT

NOLITO

FRIMON

GREESY

WHEENP

RIMPET

THE BIRTHDAY GIFTS SHE RECEIVED AT WORK WERE A PLEASANT SURPRISE, THANKS TO THE ----

Now arrange the circled letters to form the surprise answer, as suggested by the above cartoon.

Print answer here

JUMBLE®

Unscramble these six Jumbles, one letter to each square, to form six ordinary words.

WRHOGT

YASLAW

LITGUY

PIAMIR

SITVEN

TOONIN

After this inning.

When do you go out onto the field?

PLAYERS ONLY

HE WAS DRESSED IN A GIANT BIRD COSTUME AND WAS ----

Now arrange the circled letters to form the surprise answer, as suggested by the above cartoon.

Print answer here

THE

JUMBLE®

Unscramble these six Jumbles, one letter to each square, to form six ordinary words.

KLEECH

LUURYN

MERCIT

SOBARB

NITUGO

NETLAD

STORE CREDIT CARD AVAILABLE

I can see you cooking gourmet meals with that range top.

Look at this one, honey! I could make anything!

Maybe we should keep looking for a while.

AFTER SEEING THE HIGH PRICES OF NEW STOVES, HER HUSBAND WANTED TO PUT THEIR PURCHASE ----

Now arrange the circled letters to form the surprise answer, as suggested by the above cartoon.

Print answer here

JUMBLE®

Unscramble these six Jumbles, one letter to each square, to form six ordinary words.

LANMYH

PROMIT

GANYEC

LIHANE

GASTIM

MUEDIT

Wow! What a great job you've done.

Outstanding!

We made them in school.

SOME OF THE EASTER DECORATIONS THEY MADE WERE ----

Now arrange the circled letters to form the surprise answer, as suggested by the above cartoon.

Print answer here

" ◯◯◯ - ◯◯◯◯◯◯◯◯◯ "

JUMBLE®

Unscramble these six Jumbles, one letter to each square, to form six ordinary words.

TNISIS

FEDONF

GALHEG

TAEUGO

DEAGAN

DUNORG

Thanks! I'm outta here!

Have a great game!

Wow! That was a home run of a sale.

Baseballs 50% OFF!

WHEN THE STORE PUT THE BASEBALLS ON SALE, THEY WERE ---

Now arrange the circled letters to form the surprise answer, as suggested by the above cartoon.

Print answer here

◯◯◯◯◯◯ , ◯◯◯◯◯◯ , ◯◯◯◯◯

JUMBLE®

Unscramble these six Jumbles, one letter to each square, to form six ordinary words.

LETVOR

HWOOLL

CAYRBB

NECLIP

HEWAIL

MADEAG

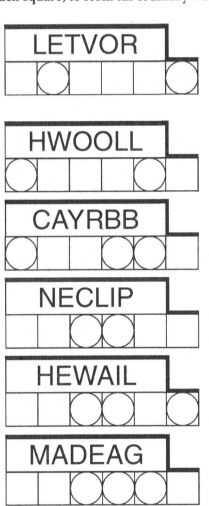

So, when you're not cutting hair, is this what you do?

It helps keep the coast looking clean.

THE BARBER WITH THE METAL DETECTOR NEAR THE SHORELINE WAS SEEN ----

Now arrange the circled letters to form the surprise answer, as suggested by the above cartoon.

Print answer here

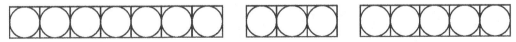

171

JUMBLE®

Unscramble these six Jumbles, one letter
to each square, to form six ordinary words.

PAWSYM

SUWINE

SLIPHO

VISLEW

DUNTIP

LENDEE

This is really depressing our property prices..

I don't know what to do.

HAPPY VALLEY

AFTER THE CITY BUILT A
LANDFILL NEXT TO THEIR
SUBDIVISION, THE
RESIDENTS WERE ----

Now arrange the circled letters to form
the surprise answer, as suggested by the
above cartoon.

Print answer here

174

JUMBLE ®

Unscramble these six Jumbles, one letter to each square, to form six ordinary words.

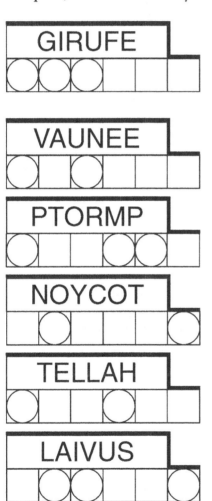

GIRUFE

VAUNEE

PTORMP

NOYCOT

TELLAH

LAIVUS

Did you even leave the house to look for a job today?

Put that down and fill these out!

Can't you fill them out for me?

WHEN IT CAME TO GETTING A JOB, THEIR SON WASN'T ---

Now arrange the circled letters to form the surprise answer, as suggested by the above cartoon.

Print answer here

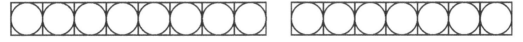

JUMBLE®

Unscramble these six Jumbles, one letter to each square, to form six ordinary words.

NUTUMA

GUHENO

TOCREK

WINDOS

FLAMEE

CLUMES

So, this is the first clock you built?

It's been years since I've seen it. Oh, the memories it brings back.

9/6

THE RETIRED CLOCKMAKER SHOWED HIS FAMILY THE CLOCK HE'D MADE ----

Now arrange the circled letters to form the surprise answer, as suggested by the above cartoon.

Print answer here

◯◯◯ ◯◯◯ ◯◯◯◯◯' ◯◯◯◯

Ok

JUMBLE

Unscramble these six Jumbles, one letter to each square, to form six ordinary words.

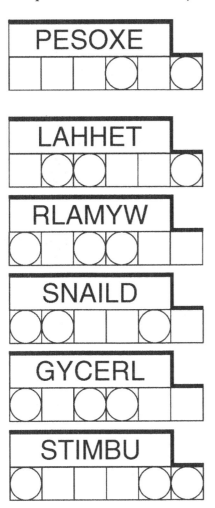

PESOXE

LAHHET

RLAMYW

SNAILD

GYCERL

STIMBU

How's the weather down there?

He just took off with it when I was at my truck.

It's happening a lot lately.

HIS HOT AIR BALLOON HAD JUST BEEN STOLEN. THE POLICEMAN TOLD HIM THAT ---

Now arrange the circled letters to form the surprise answer, as suggested by the above cartoon.

Print answer here

JUMBLE

Unscramble these six Jumbles, one letter
to each square, to form six ordinary words.

TOMFHA

SMIDOW

GISSAN

BOSWET

BBRASO

CELHNC

Welcome
Birds!
62nd Annual
Convention

No messing
around.
I came
straight here.

I see we're all here
ahead of the
crowds again.

THE BIRDS ARRIVED
RIGHT ON TIME BECAUSE
THEY WENT ----

Now arrange the circled letters to form
the surprise answer, as suggested by the
above cartoon.

Print answer here

JUMBLE®

Unscramble these six Jumbles, one letter to each square, to form six ordinary words.

DAUNOB

MARACE

TIENYT

DUNSED

PICCHU

LERONL

I can't believe we came all this way for this. Look at them celebrate.

AFTER THEIR TEAM WON THE SUPER BOWL, SOME OF THE FANS WERE ----

Now arrange the circled letters to form the surprise answer, as suggested by the above cartoon.

Print answer here

JUMBLE®

Unscramble these six Jumbles, one letter to each square, to form six ordinary words.

BLUEMM

XAHEEL

LOVTIE

KANWEE

ROTFOG

BALDEB

I had them do something special for my someone special.

ORDER HERE

This is so sweet!

HE HAD A FOAM HEART PUT ON HER COFFEE DRINK BECAUSE HE ----

Now arrange the circled letters to form the surprise answer, as suggested by the above cartoon.

Print answer here

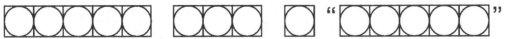

JUMBLE

Unscramble these six Jumbles, one letter to each square, to form six ordinary words.

CHIPCU

CRANEP

TOSHOE

HERDIN

SAFIOC

CATEKP

WELCOME CLASS OF 1986

Take off the cap. Let's see if you're going gray yet.

Uh, no. I didn't have time to wash my hair today.

I remember when you had hair like that.

THE MAN WAS LOSING HIS HAIR, BUT HE WANTED TO ----

Now arrange the circled letters to form the surprise answer, as suggested by the above cartoon.

Print answer here

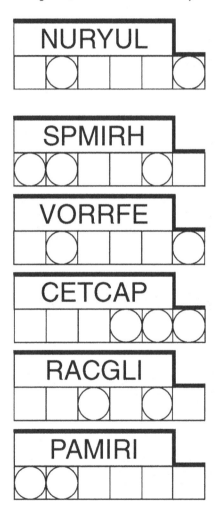

JUMBLE

Unscramble these six Jumbles, one letter to each square, to form six ordinary words.

NURYUL

SPMIRH

VORRFE

CETCAP

RACGLI

PAMIRI

I saw from afar
The smoke of a cigar
From a friend I did not know
I went to say "How do you do?"
He said, "Would you like one too?"
Then our friendship started to grow.

Jolly good, sir.

WHEN THE U.K. POLITICAL LEADER WROTE A POEM, HE WAS THE ---

Now arrange the circled letters to form the surprise answer, as suggested by the above cartoon.

Print answer here

"◯-◯◯◯◯◯" ◯◯◯◯◯◯◯◯◯

 PUZZLE 179

JUMBLE

Unscramble these six Jumbles, one letter to each square, to form six ordinary words.

TORHET

WHOOLL

ROCSHU

FIDARA

GURLFA

PROTYH

THEY WOULD BE GOING OUT TO EAT FOR SURE, BUT WHERE WAS ----

Now arrange the circled letters to form the surprise answer, as suggested by the above cartoon.

Print answer here

Answers

1. **Jumbles:** ARDOR CHAIR BLUING IMPUGN
Answer: That stingy golfer left the caddie this—
HOLDING THE BAG

2. **Jumbles:** FOAMY VOUCH DEBATE ASTRAY
Answer: A crustacean is another creature that might have this—A CRAB FOR A MATE

3. **Jumbles:** CAKED WEDGE BISECT HEREBY
Answer: This key has been known to unlock the tongue—
"WHIS-KEY"

4. **Jumbles:** SQUAB CHAOS BELFRY UNIQUE
Answer: One woman's hobby might be another woman's this—
HUBBY

5. **Jumbles:** EXPEL MUSIC LIKELY STUDIO
Answer: Runs across the floor although can't walk—
SPILLED MILK

6. **Jumbles:** SORRY LATCH BECKON PUDDLE
Answer: What David decided to do when Goliath started looking tired—"ROCK" HIM TO SLEEP

7. **Jumbles:** BULLY GIANT SONATA DEMURE
Answer: He promised first that he would be this—
TRUE TO THE LAST

8. **Jumbles:** BEIGE HASTY STUCCO PAROLE
Answer: A pea-soupy fog may give motorists this—
THE "CREEPS"

9. **Jumbles:** FOCUS MAGIC HARBOR GHETTO
Answer: Might also be "fired"—even when seemingly this—A BIG "SHOT"

10. **Jumbles:** SOAPY MAUVE FROTHY TRIPLE
Answer: The younger generation always seems more outrageous when one is no longer this—A PART OF IT

11. **Jumbles:** LOFTY THICK SADIST PILLAR
Answer: What he got as a result of careless driving—
A "LIP LASH"

12. **Jumbles:** FLOUR TOPAZ WHEEZE HALVED
Answer: That wiseacre has the solution to every difficult problem right in this—THE HOLLOW OF HIS HEAD

13. **Jumbles:** BARON NIECE SYLVAN POROUS
Answer: "What kind of marks did you get in physical education?"—"ONLY A FEW BRUISES"

14. **Jumbles:** OBESE BUSHY HAMMER INTACT
Answer: If horseback riding becomes an "addiction," this can be expensive—THE "HABIT"

15. **Jumbles:** TWILL GUILD BEGONE HORROR
Answer: The groom was fit to be tied—DOWN

16. **Jumbles:** GUISE POUND KNIGHT EXEMPT
Answer: Their involvement with diving was only this—
SKIN-DEEP

17. **Jumbles:** DROOP PURGE NORMAL UNFAIR
Answer: A theater owner never suffers in this—
THE "LONG RUN"

18. **Jumbles:** CEASE LIMIT CATNIP RANCOR
Answer: What those old-fashioned stockyards used to have about them—A CERTAIN "AIR"

19. **Jumbles:** TRULY SWOON BEHALF INLAND
Answer: What many dry speeches are—ALL WET

20. **Jumbles:** UNIFY TWEAK COHORT NUDISM
Answer: Think before you speak. Then—YOU WON'T

21. **Jumbles:** AHEAD BURST PEPTIC HANDED
Answer: The doctor said the patient's heart was this—
OFF THE "BEATIN'" PATH

22. **Jumbles:** DOGMA TARDY ACHING PESTLE
Answer: The best weight lifters—CALORIES

23. **Jumbles:** PUPIL CABIN GASKET BUCKET
Answer: When all is said and done, some people just do this—
KEEP ON TALKING

24. **Jumbles:** CHUTE SWOOP DAHLIA THEORY
Answer: He's the "master in his own home just as long as he does this—WHAT HE'S TOLD

25. **Jumbles:** AGENT SCOUT WINTRY HAWKER
Answer: Money can be lost in more this—
WAYS THAN "WON"

26. **Jumbles:** AVAIL TRAIT BANGLE COMEDY
Answer: They said the movie had a happy ending because everyone was this—GLAD IT WAS OVER

27. **Jumbles:** DINER MADAM GIGGLE ORPHAN
Answer: What that eccentric door-to-door salesman must have been—A "DING-DONG"

28. **Jumbles:** CURVE WALTZ SLUICE OBTUSE
Answer: He dines with the upper set, and is apt to do this, too—USE HIS LOWERS

29. **Jumbles:** GRAIN MOUTH DOUBLE HITHER
Answer: What the guy who was her "ideal" became after they got married—HER ORDEAL

30. **Jumbles:** HOVEL GUIDE SAFARI TURTLE
Answer: Why he took the screens off his windows—
TO LET THE FLIES OUT

31. **Jumbles:** PUPPY FEVER BEAGLE ENSIGN
Answer: The only time that crook's on the level is when he's this—SLEEPING

32. **Jumbles:** BARGE AZURE DABBLE YELLOW
Answer: He wanted to become a lawyer badly, but ended up becoming this—A BAD LAWYER

33. **Jumbles:** PERKY HOLLY GRASSY ELEVEN
Answer: Any man who argues with his wife and wins— LOSES

34. **Jumbles:** IVORY EIGHT WEEVIL TANDEM
Answer: When you "live it up," you might try to do this afterwards—LIVE IT DOWN

35. **Jumbles:** ESSAY AISLE BENIGN STODGY
Answer: Where many fliers may get their basic training—
IN NESTS

36. **Jumbles:** FAUNA TITLE PEWTER COUSIN
Answer: Look out for this when approaching a fork in the road—A PUNCTURE

37. **Jumbles:** ACRID CLOAK SINFUL TUMULT
Answer: One doesn't run after this—THE LAST TRAIN

38. **Jumbles:** BRIBE TOXIN GRUBBY ASTHMA
Answer: This is right when it's left on both sides—A MARGIN

39. **Jumbles:** EAGLE DECRY IMPEND AFRAID
Answer: What an experienced rider might get when he falls of a horse—DE-RIDED

40. **Jumbles:** CRAZE ANKLE MELODY BUTLER
Answer: You don't appreciate the usefulness of this until you use it up—AN UMBRELLA

41. **Jumbles:** FELON AMUSE SPORTY NUMBER
Answer: What experienced gossips often depend on—
THEIR SENSE OF RUMOR

42. **Jumbles:** CRACK SMOKY CORRAL KETTLE
Answer: Why the escaped con on the lam took a job on the railroad—TO MAKE TRACKS

43. **Jumbles:** CABLE AWARD SAFARI PENCIL
Answer: What the royal parent was tempted to call his newborn heir—PRINCE OF "WAILS"

44. **Jumbles:** ARDOR OBESE PRIMER BLOODY
Answer: What a dieter without will power is—A POOR LOSER

45. **Jumbles:** CRIME SCARF HEARSE ANGINA
Answer: How the Englishman described his wife's driving—"SMASHING!"

46. **Jumbles:** HUMID MIRTH FIGURE EYELID
Answer: What the newlywed music lovers pledged each other—HIGH FIDELITY

47. **Jumbles:** BURLY MUSIC FUTILE HANDED
Answer: How the potter makes his living—HE "URNS" IT

48. **Jumbles:** BARGE LANKY SLEIGH PICKET
Answer: What a pessimist might expect to get on a silver platter—TARNISH

49. **Jumbles:** CLOVE AHEAD BESIDE PASTRY
Answer: What the playwright turned gardener worked on—HIS PLOT

50. **Jumbles:** SUITE MERCY CRAVAT HALLOW
Answer: What the baseball player turned orchestra leader had to know—THE SCORE

51. **Jumbles:** AVAIL BOWER HAMMER BEWAIL
Answer: How you might announce the birth of a son to your friends—BY "HEIR" MAIL

52. **Jumbles:** MAGIC SNORT BLEACH PERSON
Answer: What she said when he yelled at her about the money she spent on a cashmere coat—"IT'S MERE CASH!"

53. **Jumbles:** ADMIT HITCH GEYSER NATURE
Answer: What the horse thought his wife looked like as she prepared for bed—A NIGHT-MARE

54. **Jumbles:** MOURN BUSHY MUTTON DELUGE
Answer: What the bored percussion player thought his work was—HUMDRUM

55. **Jumbles:** AROMA STOOP BUSILY DEMISE
Answer: What the lowest voice in the prison quartet was—A STRIPED BASS

56. **Jumbles:** MOLDY ADULT GOSPEL CIPHER
Answer: What the butcher's son had when his dad got locked in the refrigerator—A COLD POP

57. **Jumbles:** CHALK CHESS BODILY POPLIN
Answer: Where was the fish when the kid playing hooky caught him—IN A SCHOOL

58. **Jumbles:** PLUME AMITY DETACH LUNACY
Answer: What the waiter did when asked how the seafood was—HE CLAMMED UP

59. **Jumbles:** FRAUD TEASE INJURY COUGAR
Answer: What the romantic Spaniard picked in his sweetheart's garden—A GUITAR

60. **Jumbles:** TRIPE PAPER ADVICE DECENT
Answer: How hair that was parted yesterday may appear today—DEPARTED

61. **Jumbles:** SCOUR JUDGE LAUNCH POSTAL
Answer: What the comical surgeon was—AN OLD CUTUP

62. **Jumbles:** NOTCH DROOP IMPEDE GENIUS
Answer: What the necktie salesmen did at their convention—TIED ONE ON

63. **Jumbles:** LEAFY BOOTH EFFACE WALRUS
Answer: What the weather forecasters sometimes are—ALL WET

64. **Jumbles:** MADLY MAIZE SNITCH DENOTE
Answer: What the hay fever sufferer did when he read about the pollen count—SNEEZED AT IT

65. **Jumbles:** RAVEN HEFTY PALACE FACILE
Answer: What the seasoned commuter tries when he forgets his ticket—"FARE PLAY"

66. **Jumbles:** TOXIC COUPE BONNET FORAGE
Answer: Another name for a check forger—A NO-ACCOUNT

67. **Jumbles:** BULLY PARCH INFLUX AMBUSH
Answer: What the inebriated insect was—A BAR FLY

68. **Jumbles:** FEVER BORAX ARTERY SLEEPY
Answer: What the redcap who went into foreign trade was—AN EX-PORTER

69. **Jumbles:** FORUM BISON GOBLET COOKIE
Answer: What happened when the thermometer fell on a hot day?—IT BROKE

70. **Jumbles:** GIANT AGONY CABANA CONCUR
Answer: What the French cabaret dancer kept insisting—I CAN CANCAN

71. **Jumbles:** ASSAY NUDGE RATHER THROAT
Answer: Always cheered when they're down and out—ASTRONAUTS

72. **Jumbles:** PUDGY GOING BICEPS DIVERT
Answer: He hoped to make a big splash with the ladies but turned out to be this—A BIG DRIP

73. **Jumbles:** ODIUM HOUSE FORGET TOUCHY
Answer: What the shoe merchant did about his bills—HE FOOTED THEM

74. **Jumbles:** JETTY FORTY STOLEN BEFORE
Answer: How the tenderfoot felt after his first day on horseback—BETTER OFF

75. **Jumbles:** BARON LATCH FEWEST AWEIGH
Answer: What the werewolf said when she asked for mink—"WEAR WOLF!"

76. **Jumbles:** HELLO FAIRY DRUDGE IMBIBE
Answer: What the passengers did to the conductor when the train was late—"RAILED" AT HIM

77. **Jumbles:** ELDER MUSTY IMMUNE HAPPEN
Answer: They make holdups easier—HANDLES

78. **Jumbles:** CHIDE EXUDE MUSCLE REALTY
Answer: The kind of clothes you might buy after you've lost weight—"REDUCED"

79. **Jumbles:** TACKY HONEY ACHING PURPLE
Answer: This could save a high-up from a painful comedown—A PARACHUTE

80. **Jumbles:** HAVOC MINUS BRUTAL STYMIE
Answer: A loud cry that's quiet to start with—"SH-OUT"

81. **Jumbles:** TOKEN BURLY DECENT DISMAL
Answer: What the lottery-winning Realtor considered his property purchase—"LOTS" OF LUCK

82. **Jumbles:** SAUTE CURVE BELFRY DEVICE
Answer: When they watched the steelworkers the crowd was—RIVETED

83. **Jumbles:** CHALK PROVE FORGET HORROR
Answer: What the cop moonlighting as an actor was known as—A REAL TROOPER

84. **Jumbles:** BOGUS CHIME GOLFER PUNDIT
Answer: What the runner wanted to get a jump on—THE HURDLES

85. **Jumbles:** HYENA METAL HICCUP DISCUS
Answer: This can rescue a meal when all else fails—SALT, IN A PINCH

86. **Jumbles:** MOUTH FORTY DARING WEASEL
Answer: Authoring spooky stories made him this—A "GHOST" WRITER

87. **Jumbles:** CABIN CLOUT COERCE DISMAY
Answer: Why the bank robbers headed for the seashore—THE COAST WAS CLEAR

88. **Jumbles:** CHEEK EXULT FEWEST VERIFY
Answer: How he felt when his car ran out of gas—FUEL-ISH

89. **Jumbles:** TRILL EXUDE AFRAID BODILY
Answer: What the landscaper uncovered in the royal garden—THE REAL DIRT

90. **Jumbles:** FLAKE ELEGY CORRAL RITUAL
Answer: What the birds gave the nature lovers—A REAL TRILL

91. **Jumbles:** AGONY DOUBT BALSAM DRUDGE
Answer: The purse snatcher's favorite activity at a party—THE GRAB BAG

92. **Jumbles:** DROOP TACKY YEOMAN POSTAL
Answer: People who believe in the fountain of youth get this—SOAKED

93. **Jumbles:** PUDGY AMITY THWART DOMINO
Answer: An ambitious cowboy's life is filled with this—GIDDAP and WHOA

94. **Jumbles:** AROMA TOXIC FATHOM HAMPER
Answer: What the well-to-do stockbroker gave the maitre d'—A HOT TIP

95. **Jumbles:** BELLE NAVAL SNITCH FEMALE
Answer: What the cops considered the strong-arm robber—A MAN OF STEAL

96. **Jumbles:** DEITY FRAUD FOMENT TYPHUS
Answer: What the post office experiences when the rates are about to go up—A STAMP-EDE

97. **Jumbles:** CRESS POWER FARINA COUGAR
Answer: Why the pilot couldn't decide where to land—HE WAS UP IN THE AIR

98. **Jumbles:** DIZZY KITTY MOTIVE HOPPER
Answer: What the shady car dealer did to his customer—TOOK HIM FOR A RIDE

99. **Jumbles:** CHIDE MADLY TANDEM TYRANT
Answer: What the elegantly dressed repairman was known as—A HANDY ANDY

100. **Jumbles:** QUEUE PIPER TURGID NOZZLE
Answer: How the coffee shop owner made his money—HE URNED IT

101. **Jumbles:** GLADE GIZMO DIGEST INVOKE
Answer: He got a job building a moat, but he wasn't—DIGGING IT

102. **Jumbles:** BURLY STAND NOVICE POETIC
Answer: People enjoy playing Jumble on a regular basis because it's—"PUN" TO SOLVE

103. **Jumbles:** PETTY JUNKY DISMAY POUNCE
Answer: He wanted to get the skunk out of the garage, but the skunk—PUT UP A STINK

104. **Jumbles:** VALID PRESS SNITCH BURLAP
Answer: He wanted to open a junkyard in the neighborhood, but he had to—SCRAP HIS PLANS

105. **Jumbles:** COACH HEFTY GOSSIP IMPORT
Answer: The cow who was always borrowing money was a—MOOCHER

106. **Jumbles:** ADOPT CLING INFECT BONNET
Answer: Trying to eat outside with a thunderstorm approaching was—NO PICNIC

107. **Jumbles:** MUGGY AWAIT LONELY MISERY
Answer: The construction of their new pool had gone—SWIMMINGLY

108. **Jumbles:** SWORN HUMID STOOGE CODDLE
Answer: These birds of prey met late in the evening because they were—NIGHT OWLS

109. **Jumbles:** WEARY KNELT MUTTON AFFECT
Answer: The clumsy horse didn't do well at the dance class because he had—TWO LEFT FEET

110. **Jumbles:** MONTH WHIRL OUTBID JANGLE
Answer: The table had been reserved for a party of eight, and the waitress was—WAITING ON THEM

111. **Jumbles:** CEASE CROAK MANNER BRUNCH
Answer: How much did the pirate pay for the corn?—A BUCK AN EAR

112. **Jumbles:** LEAKY MADLY DOUGHY JABBER
Answer: When the "punny" puzzle makers went out to eat, they enjoyed the—"JUMBLE-AYA"

113. **Jumbles:** MERCY TITLE BATTER UNWIND
Answer: Charging so many things on his credit card was—"DEBT-TRIMENTAL"

114. **Jumbles:** ANKLE KUDOS DEPUTY ANYHOW
Answer: The bread company's top secret recipe was—"KNEAD" TO KNOW

115. **Jumbles:** COMIC TENTH FINISH PLEDGE
Answer: When it came to choosing wrought iron or chain link, they were—ON THE FENCE

116. **Jumbles:** SHOVE GOING TICKET AVENUE
Answer: The driver, with the bad cold, wasn't happy with all the—CONGESTION

117. **Jumbles:** PRICE TANGY WISDOM SHAKEN
Answer: He was hoping his mother-in-law would be leaving today, but she had—STAYING POWER

118. **Jumbles:** TRUNK WHEAT GLOOMY BOUNTY
Answer: The new one-story house for sale at the bottom of the Grand Canyon was a—BUNGA-LOW

119. **Jumbles:** PICKY HONEY CACTUS REDUCE
Answer: When the hen bought the new two-door sports car, she bought a—CHICKEN "COUPE"

120. **Jumbles:** RAINY MUGGY WINERY THROAT
Answer: The dog just couldn't finish chewing the whole bone, and it was—GNAWING AT HIM

121. **Jumbles:** DECAY RAINY LOVING BABIED
Answer: He couldn't afford a lot of property to grow wine grapes, so he settled for a—VINE-YARD

122. **Jumbles:** ODDLY BROIL FREEZE FAUCET
Answer: After the explosion at the French cheese factory, there was—A LOT OF "DE-BRIE"

123. **Jumbles:** ACUTE RIVER BLIGHT ALLIED
Answer: After gaining independence from Britain, their favorite beverage was—"LIBER-TEA"

124. **Jumbles:** WEDGE ROUND CATCHY JUNGLE
Answer: The submarine was brand-new and the captain was anxious to—GET UNDERWAY

125. **Jumbles:** CHEWY MINUS EXCESS RODENT
Answer: He wanted his glasses to be unlike anyone else's, so he had a pair—"CUSTOM-EYES-ED"

126. **Jumbles:** TANGY SEEDY MATTER APPEAL
Answer: The popularity of word processors in the 1960s led to—MANY TYPES

127. **Jumbles:** HOUSE LOFTY RADIAL ROOKIE
Answer: Barbie was expensive, so they hoped she'd settle for the—"DOLL-HER" STORE

128. **Jumbles:** PLAID CYCLE MISFIT AMBUSH
Answer: When the wind stopped, he told everyone on the sailboat to—STAY CALM

129. **Jumbles:** RATIO SLANT GERBIL CREAKY
Answer: On the sci-fi schow, the Milky Way had a—STARRING ROLE

130. **Jumbles:** SHYLY ERUPT ONWARD FUTURE
Answer: She had so many clothes, that her home looked like a—"WEAR-HOUSE"

131. **Jumbles:** REBEL RIGID VACANT UNLOAD
Answer: When it came to measuring the Earth's circumference, there was a—LEARNING CURVE

132. **Jumbles:** SUSHI DINKY TRIPLE FEMALE
Answer: The housefly and the cockroach were—"PEST" FRIENDS

133. **Jumbles:** ELDER FLOOD EXHALE FLOPPY
Answer: Granny Smith's grandson was the—APPLE OF HER EYE

134. **Jumbles:** MUSTY MOVIE WRITER FACADE
Answer: The archer's new cologne was—"ARROW-MATIC"

135. **Jumbles:** KNOWN ONION WICKED CASINO
Answer: The woodpecker hoped the tree would be home for a long time,—KNOCK ON WOOD

136. **Jumbles:** PICKY KNIFE DONKEY OUTLET
Answer: When Steve Martin got the role of Inspector Clouseau, he was—TICKLED PINK

186

137. **Jumbles:** QUASH UTTER ENOUGH GLITZY
Answer: The brilliant ophthalmologist had a—HIGH "EYE"Q

138. **Jumbles:** UNDUE SUSHI ABRUPT HOOPLA
Answer: She hadn't painted in years, so she took a class to—BRUSH UP ON IT

139. **Jumbles:** SWIFT AGENT AMOEBA SURELY
Answer: When the scuba diver startled the octopus, it put him—IN "ARMS" WAY

140. **Jumbles:** OUNCE WHILE PADDLE ABSORB
Answer: Their tour of the Grand Canyon began with their guide saying—"LOW" AND BEHOLD

141. **Jumbles:** VIRUS TITLE CABANA MIRROR
Answer: When fans from opposing teams got off the plane, it was—"A-RIVAL" TIME

142. **Jumbles:** WHIRL DITTO FLAUNT DEVOUR
Answer: Aliens decided to take over Earth because they thought—THE WORLD OF IT

143. **Jumbles:** FORGO GUMBO WALNUT FUSION
Answer: The talkative person wrapping Christmas presents at the mall had the—GIFT OF GAB

144. **Jumbles:** HYENA MOGUL BUNDLE CAMERA
Answer: When it came ot making money selling grapes, the grower—MADE A BUNCH

145. **Jumbles:** THANK NUDGE CREAMY DISMAL
Answer: Once ranked #1 for 302 straight weeks, Roger Federer was—UNMATCHED

146. **Jumbles:** SILKY GLITZ NUMBER PARDON
Answer: "Harry Potter" fans couldn't put the books down, finding them—SPELLBINDING

147. **Jumbles:** GRANT AHEAD BODILY ADMIRE
Answer: After test-driving the car, they were ready to drive a—HARD BARGAIN

148. **Jumbles:** ADAPT EXACT MIDDAY MIDDLE
Answer: With great restaurants in Milan, Florence and Rome, they enjoyed their trip to—"EATALY"

149. **Jumbles:** LINER GAMUT TATTLE FERRET
Answer: She couldn't eat another bite, and everyone else was in—FULL AGREEMENT

150. **Jumbles:** MERGE GIZMO WEEKLY PANTRY
Answer: When ancient Italians built human-powered ships, they created a—"ROW-MEN" EMPIRE

151. **Jumbles:** LATCH WATCH LONELY LEEWAY
Answer: When the carpet store had a huge sale, customers were—WALL-TO-WALL

152. **Jumbles:** GRILL SKIMP FACADE COLUMN
Answer: The number of customers rose at the skydiving school, thanks to their—FALLING PRICES

153. **Jumbles:** FLOSS IMAGE NIMBLE FERVOR
Answer: With planes landing one after another, the sky was filled with—AIR LINES

154. **Jumbles:** FETCH IDIOT ONWARD INFANT
Answer: He wanted to expand his collection, and the Mesopotamian abacus would make a—NICE ADDITION

155. **Jumbles:** STASH CLING DEPICT ORNERY
Answer: The lumberjack could chop through a piece of wood in a—SPLIT SECOND

156. **Jumbles:** FOAMY INEPT BETTER ADJUST
Answer: They were able to set up at the campground after paying an—"ADMIT-TENTS" FEE

157. **Jumbles:** SHOVE CHUNK CELERY BOXING
Answer: No one told her what to purchase. She did her own research and was there—"BUY" CHOICE

158. **Jumbles:** CRIMP ANNOY POLLEN BUCKET
Answer: She grew and harvested her own food because she was a—PICKY EATER

159. **Jumbles:** BRAVO DOUBT NINETY LOUNGE
Answer: The African felines were exhausted after a long day and were just—"LION" AROUND

160. **Jumbles:** CLOAK BLOOM EMBARK REMOVE
Answer: He remembered inventing the "DRAM" computer chip in 1968 because it was—MEMORABLE

161. **Jumbles:** DEFECT TOPPLE THWART EITHER REFUSE ABLAZE
Answer: The post office in Washington, D.C., featured—CAPITAL LETTERS

162. **Jumbles:** MAYHEM SHOULD GARLIC FEWEST NINETY MARKET
Answer: When the attorney became a partner, he received—FIRM HANDSHAKES

163. **Jumbles:** CANOPY GALLON DOLLAR MISERY PRANCE MODEST
Answer: He enjoyed being a father all week long, but he was especially enjoying—"SON-DAY" MORNING

164. **Jumbles:** SPLASH BEHIND UNPAID TALLER INSIST UNLESS
Answer: The TV show "Seinfeld" has been so successful in syndication thanks to—REPEAT BUSINESS

165. **Jumbles:** ACCENT LOTION INFORM GEYSER NEPHEW PERMIT
Answer: The birthday gifts she received at work were a pleasant surprise, thanks to the—PRESENT COMPANY

166. **Jumbles:** GROWTH ALWAYS GUILTY IMPAIR INVEST NOTION
Answer: He was dressed in a giant bird costume and was—WAITING IN THE WINGS

167. **Jumbles:** HECKLE UNRULY METRIC ABSORB OUTING DENTAL
Answer: After seeing the high prices of new stoves, her husband wanted to put their purchase—ON THE BACK BURNER

168. **Jumbles:** HYMNAL IMPORT AGENCY INHALE STIGMA TEDIUM
Answer: Some of the Easter decorations they made were—"EGG-CEPTIONAL"

169. **Jumbles:** INSIST OFFEND HAGGLE OUTAGE AGENDA GROUND
Answer: When the store put the baseballs on sale, they were—GOING, GOING, GONE

170. **Jumbles:** REVOLT HOLLOW CRABBY PENCIL AWHILE DAMAGE
Answer: The barber with the metal detector near the shoreline was seen—COMBING THE BEACH

171. **Jumbles:** SWAMPY UNWISE POLISH SWIVEL PUNDIT NEEDLE
Answer: After the city built a landfill next to their subdivision, the residents were—DOWN IN THE DUMPS

172. **Jumbles:** FIGURE AVENUE PROMPT TYCOON LETHAL VISUAL
Answer: When it came to getting a job, their son wasn't—APPLYING HIMSELF

173. **Jumbles:** AUTUMN ENOUGH ROCKET DISOWN FEMALE MUSCLE
Answer: The retired clockmaker showed his family the clock he'd made—FOR OLD TIME'S SAKE

174. **Jumbles:** EXPOSE HEALTH WARMLY ISLAND CLERGY SUBMIT
Answer: His hot air balloon had just been stolen. The policeman told him that—CRIME WAS ON THE RISE

175. **Jumbles:** FATHOM WISDOM ASSIGN BESTOW ABSORB CLENCH
Answer: The birds arrived right on time because they went—AS THE CROW FLIES

176. **Jumbles:** ABOUND CAMERA ENTITY SUDDEN HICCUP ENROLL
Answer: After their team won the Super Bowl, some of the fans were—IN "ATTEND-DANCE"

177. **Jumbles:** MUMBLE EXHALE VIOLET WEAKEN FORGOT DABBLE
Answer: He had a foam heart put on her coffee drink because he—LOVED HER A "LATTE"

178. **Jumbles:** HICCUP PRANCE SOOTHE HINDER FIASCO PACKET
Answer: The man was losing his hair, but he wanted to—KEEP IT UNDER HIS HAT

179. **Jumbles:** UNRULY SHRIMP FERVOR ACCEPT GARLIC IMPAIR
Answer: When the U.K. political leader wrote a poem, he was the—"P-RHYME" MINISTER

180. **Jumbles:** HOTTER HOLLOW CHORUS AFRAID FRUGAL TROPHY
Answer: They would be going out to eat for sure, but where was—FOOD FOR THOUGHT